Small Business

A Step-by-Step A... ...
Products and Services Online

[a Rapid Business Growth Guide]

Dan Braun and Patch Baker

Rocketeer.Press
Matthews, NC

Copyright @ 2023 by Dan Braun and Patch Baker. All rights reserved worldwide. Published in the United States by XTRA EDGE LLC dba Rocketeer.Press, Matthews, North Carolina.

Cover design: Afzal Hossain
Images (cover and interior): licensed from Adobe Stock
Editor: Michelle C. Braun
RPIID: 325140

No part of this publication may be reproduced, stored in a retrieval system, or transmitted in any form or by any means, electronic, mechanical, photocopying, recording, scanning, or otherwise, except for "fair use" as brief quotations embodied in articles and reviews, without the prior written permission of the Publisher. Requests to the Publisher for permission should be addressed to the Permissions Department, Rocketeer.Press, 2217 Matthews Township Pkwy, Ste D-233, Matthews, NC 28105.

The Rapid Business Growth Guide and the Rocket logo are trademarks of XTRA EDGE LLC and/or its affiliates in the United States and other countries and may not be used without written permission. All other trademarks are the property of their respective owners. All images and graphic designs used on the cover and/or in the work are owned or licensed by the publisher.

This book is a collaborative effort between the authors and ChatGPT, an AI language model developed by OpenAI. The authors have played a crucial role in providing a comprehensive outline and framework for the book, ensuring that the content is relevant, engaging, and in line with their vision. While ChatGPT has generated a significant portion of the content based on the authors' guidance, it is important to note that the AI-generated material has been thoroughly reviewed, edited, and curated by the authors themselves. This rigorous process was undertaken to ensure accuracy, authenticity, and adherence to the highest standards of quality. The collaboration between the authors and ChatGPT aims to offer readers a unique, informative, and enjoyable reading experience, combining the strengths of human expertise and AI-generated content.

While the publisher and authors have used their best efforts in preparing this book, they make no representations or warranties with respect to the accuracy or completeness of the contents of this book and specifically disclaim any implied warranties of merchantability or fitness for a particular purpose. No warranty may be created or extended by sales representatives or written, audio, or video sales media. The advice and strategies contained herein may not be suitable for your situation. Always consult with a professional before acting on any information included in this publication. Further, be aware that websites and other resources listed in this work may have changed or disappeared between the time this work was written and when it is read. Neither the publisher nor the authors shall be liable for any loss of profit or other commercial damage, including but not limited to special, incidental, consequential, or other damages.

For general information on our other products and services, please contact us via our website at https://www.RapidBusinessGrowth.co or by sending a letter to Rapid Business Growth c/o Rocketeer.Press, 2217 Matthews Township Pkwy, Ste D-233, Matthews, NC 28105 USA.

To all the courageous small business owners, your entrepreneurial spirit, commitment to innovation, and dedication to making a difference are truly inspiring.

Thank you.

CONTENTS

INTRODUCTION 1

HOW TO USE THIS GUIDE 3

CHAPTER 1: How Defining Your Target Market Gives You A Clear Competitive Advantage 5

Chapter 2: How Conducting Market Research Helps You Create Products And Services Customers Want 18

Chapter 3: How Developing Your Brand Identity Helps You Increase Customer Loyalty And Eliminate The Competition 29

Chapter 4: How Setting Marketing Goals And Objectives Can Skyrocket Sales 41

CHAPTER 5: Developing A Marketing Plan To Successfully Promote Your Product Or Service Online 53

Chapter 6: How To Create Powerful Marketing Messages That Command Attention And Boost Sales 64

Chapter 7: Why Using Social Media For Marketing Is The Ultimate Game Changer 76

Chapter 8: How To Create Successful Email Marketing Campaigns That Convert 90

Chapter 9: Why Content Engagement Should Be A Top Priority For Your Small Business 105

Chapter 10: How To Implement Website Search Engine Optimization As A Cost-Effective Way To Attract New Customers 117

Chapter 11: How To Measure Marketing Results To Fine-Tune Your Messaging And Increase Conversion Rates 130

Chapter 12: How Continuously Improving Your Online Marketing Strategy Boosts Your Business Growth 142

Final Thoughts 155

About The Authors 156

INTRODUCTION

Welcome to "Small Business Marketing: A Step-by-Step Action Plan for Selling Products and Services Online"!

Let's face it... As a small business owner, you wear too many hats.

You're the CEO, operations manager, HR manager, bookkeeper, bill collector, customer service rep, social media manager, event planner, sales rep, copywriter, trainer, coach, and marketing specialist all rolled into one.

Whew!

Of all those roles, marketing is often one of the first things that gets pushed to the back burner or ignored entirely.

It's perfectly understandable... Many small business owners struggle with knowing where to start, how to allocate limited resources, and how to measure the success of their efforts.

Yet marketing is *critically* important to the success of your business.

Effective marketing campaigns help you build brand recognition and awareness, generate leads, and convert those leads into paying customers — often on autopilot, 24 hours a day, 7 days a week, 365 days a year!

Without a strong marketing strategy in place, it's difficult to reach new customers and keep the existing ones engaged.

But there are still many misconceptions surrounding marketing, including "it's too expensive", "it takes too much time", and "it's too hard to learn".

As a result, small business owners often find themselves feeling stuck and uncertain about the next steps to take to grow their business.

This is where this guide comes in.

We wrote this to help you overcome the common hurdles and frustrations of marketing. It provides you with a clear, actionable plan for building and growing a successful business.

Throughout the pages of this guide, you'll learn about various aspects of marketing, including defining your target market, developing a marketing plan, branding, social media, and more.

You'll also discover tools and strategies to help you make the most of your marketing efforts, no matter your budget.

Whether you're a seasoned entrepreneur or just starting out, by the time you reach the end of this guide, you'll have the confidence (and step-by-step instructions) to take control of your marketing and turn your vision for your business into a reality.

One of the key focuses of this guide is on cost-effective marketing methods.

We understand that small businesses often operate on a tight budget, which is why we provide tips and tricks for maximizing your marketing dollars.

And if you're willing to put in the time, many of the strategies you'll learn don't cost any money at all, such as search engine optimization (SEO) and social media marketing.

Another important aspect of this guide is teaching you how to measure your marketing success.

Without metrics, it's difficult to know what's working and what's not. We'll help you understand the key metrics to track and how to use them to make informed decisions about your marketing strategy.

The journey to building a successful small business can be challenging, but it doesn't have to be.

"Small Business Marketing: A Step-by-Step Action Plan for Selling Products and Services Online" is your roadmap to success.

With our clear, step-by-step approach, you'll be able to overcome the common obstacles and challenges that most small business owners face when it comes to marketing.

So buckle up, grab a coffee (or whatever your favorite beverage might be), and get ready to take your marketing game — and your business — to the next level!

HOW TO USE THIS GUIDE

This is *not* your typical business book.

It's a GUIDE that cuts straight to the chase in every chapter.

You're here because you need to grow your business, like, yesterday. Right?

We respect that, and so we're not going to waste your time with long-winded soliloquies that take up the first half of most marketing books.

Instead, we've structured this Guide as a 90-day program with 12 chapters spread over 12 weeks.

Follow the Guide by going through one chapter a week, then TAKE ACTION on what you've learned.

Keep in mind that knowledge is only useful if you take action. *Action* is the true power.

Action informed by knowledge is a SUPER POWER. It's where you develop "muscle memory" and where you truly understand a topic at a deeper level.

Chapter 1 is foundational for the entire Guide. It's about defining your target market, and we refer back to it often.

The rest of the chapters are designed to stand alone, so after going through Chapter 1, feel free to skip around to the chapters that are *most* important to you and your small business *right now*.

If you feel you already have mastery over a specific chapter topic, or think it doesn't apply to you, give yourself 5 minutes to skim over it first. You may pick up a thing or two that you didn't know before.

Our aim is to give you a solid foundation for each topic, but if you want to go deeper or need personalized coaching on any of these marketing strategies, please visit us at www.RapidBusinessGrowth.co.

Each chapter of "Small Business Marketing: A Step-by-Step Action Plan for Selling Products and Services Online" is divided into 7 sections.

These sections are the same in every chapter to help you easily navigate through the guide and reinforce what you've learned. The sections are:

1. **Why Is It Important?**
   We didn't pick these specific marketing strategies randomly. Here's where you learn why the current strategy is essential for your small business.

2. **"What Happens If I Don't...?"**
   Proceed with caution: This section highlights the consequences of ignoring this marketing strategy.

3. **The Essential Elements**
   There are probably a hundred considerations for every strategy, but the 90/10 Rule says you get 90% of the results from just 10% of the actions. Here, we filter down to that core 10%.

4. **Step-by-Step Instructions**
   Here's where we break the current strategy down into small, manageable chunks. We even give you suggested time limits to accomplish each step so you don't take a full day to do something that can be done in an hour or two.

5. **Specific Scenario**
   This section offers a fictional example of how a small business might implement the step-by-step instructions for this marketing strategy.

6. **Strategy Snapshot**
   This is a chapter summary designed to help you reinforce what you just learned.

7. **Take The First Step**
   Every journey begins with a single step. Here's where we provide clarity on the best way to get started.

If you read the guide all at once, it may seem repetitive because every chapter follows the same format with the same seven sections.

However, *it's not meant to be read all at once.*

This guide is designed to be read then ACTED UPON.

Action is the key to growing your business, and that's what this guide is all about.

When you get to the "Take The First Step" section, it's important that you actually put the guide down and TAKE ACTION.

Reading this guide a thousand times without implementation won't change a thing about your business.

Learn, take action daily, repeat. That's how you create rapid business growth.

===

Now you know how to use this Guide to get the most out of it.

So what are you waiting for?

Get out there and change the world!

Dan & Patch

P.S. We want to hear your success story. Tell us how you're doing after you've taken action on one or more of the strategies (or just to ask us any questions you might have) by contacting us at www.RapidBusinessGrowth.co.

CHAPTER 1:
How Defining Your Target Market Gives You A Clear Competitive Advantage

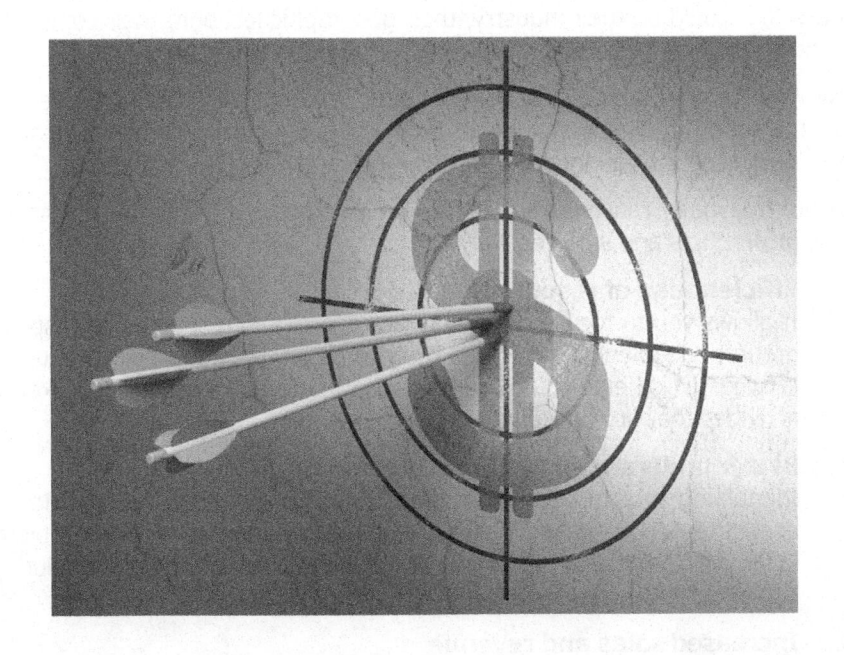

"Talent hits a target no one else can hit. Genius hits a target no one else can see."

— Arthur Schopenhauer

Why Is It Important To Define Your Target Market?

When you're running a business, it's important to know who your target market is. These are the people you want to reach with your products or services.

Your target market is made up of people or businesses who have something in common.

For people, it's things like their age, where they live, and their interests. For businesses, it could be their industry, their geographic location, their company size, and so on.

Ideally, your target market is made up of your "dream customer". In other words, the superfan who buys all your products and services, gives you 5-star reviews online, sends you lots of referrals, and rarely, if ever, complains.

There are five major reasons you need to know exactly who your target market is for your products and services:

1. **Efficient use of resources**
   It allows you to focus your marketing efforts and resources on a specific group of people who are more likely to be interested in your product or service. This helps you to avoid wasting time and money on marketing activities that are unlikely to produce results.

2. **Better understanding of customer needs**
   Identifying your target market helps you to understand the specific needs, preferences, and behaviors of your customers. You'll be able to tailor your product or service to better meet their needs and provide better customer satisfaction.

3. **Increased sales and revenue**
   By targeting a specific group of people who are more likely to be interested in your product or service, you increase the likelihood of converting them into paying customers, which can ultimately lead to increased sales and revenue.

4. **More relevant marketing messages**
   Identifying your target market helps you to create marketing messages that are more relevant to their specific needs and interests. You can communicate more effectively with your potential customers and increase the likelihood of converting them into paying customers.

5. **Competitive advantage**
   Understanding your target market better than your competitors can give you a competitive advantage. By tailoring your products and services to your target market, you can differentiate your product or service from your competitors to provide a unique selling proposition (USP).

"What Happens If I Don't Define My Target Market?"

Not having a clear understanding of your target market can have some serious consequences. Here's what you need to watch out for:

- **Wasting resources on ineffective marketing campaigns**
  Without a clear understanding of your target market, you'll end up throwing your hard-earned money down the drain on marketing campaigns that don't connect with potential customers.

- **Failing to differentiate from competitors**
  Consumers have a ton of choices these days. Without a specific target market in mind, your message will be broad and unfocused, making it difficult to attract new customers.

- **Decreased customer loyalty**
  Customers are more likely to remain loyal to a brand that understands their needs and wants. When you don't really know your target market, your customers will feel like you're not really listening to them. This inevitably leads to decreased loyalty and lost revenue.

- **Inability to develop tailored products or services**
  Do you want to create products or services that your customers will absolutely love? Of course, you do! But without a clear understanding of who they are, it will be really hard to customize solutions for them.

- **Missing out on potential growth opportunities**
  If you don't know your target market, you won't be able to serve them at the highest level. You'll miss new and evolving trends that could very well lead to expansion and growth.

===

By truly researching and understanding your target market, you will position your small business for long-term growth and success.

The Essential Elements Of Defining Your Target Market

By considering the following essential elements, you can develop a more comprehensive understanding of your target market and develop marketing strategies that are targeted and effective.

Take out a sheet of paper, or open your favorite note-taking app, and write these down. The more of these you can fill out, the closer you'll get to finding your target market.

1. **Demographics**

    - **Age:** Age often influences purchasing behavior, as different age groups have different needs, wants, and interests.

    - **Gender:** Gender also plays a role in purchasing behavior, as men, women, and non-binaries usually have different preferences and buying patterns.

    - **Income:** A customer's income level indicate their purchasing power and the types of products or services they can afford.

    - **Education:** Education level provides insight into a customer's interests, values, and decision-making style.

    - **Occupation:** A customer's occupation generally influences their buying behavior and the types of products or services they need.

    - **Ethnicity:** Ethnic background provides information about cultural values and beliefs that influence purchasing decisions.

    - **Geography:** Where customers live, including city, state, and country, provides information about their local market and competition.

    - **Family status:** Are they married, divorced, cohabiting, or living alone? Do they have children, and if so, how many and how old are they?

    - **Pet parenthood:** Do they have a dog, cat, bird, hamster, reptile, and/or aquarium, and how many of each? Do they consider their pets as companions or fur-babies?

2. **Psychographics**

    - **Personality:** Extroversion, introversion, emotional stability, openness to new experiences, conscientiousness, and agreeableness.

    - **Lifestyle:** A customer's overall way of living, such as their circle of friends, spending and saving habits, investments, the type of neighborhood they live in, how they dress, and where they frequently spend their time all provide valuable insights.

- **Values:** About what is important in life, such as family, security, environmentalism, spirituality, and personal success.
- **Attitudes:** Especially towards a particular product or brand, such as whether they view it as high quality or innovative.
- **Aptitudes:** Their intelligence level, technical skills, and artistic abilities.
- **Interests:** Different than hobbies, which is what they do, interests are more about what they like to learn or consume. They may love to watch baking shows, for example, but never bake anything.
- **Beliefs:** Religious views, political views, code of ethics, outlook on life, assumptions about the world and others.

3. **Behaviors**

    - **Hobbies:** A customer's hobbies, such as outdoor activities, technology, or cooking.
    - **Purchasing habits:** How often they buy products or services, what they buy, and how much they are willing to spend.
    - **Brand loyalty:** Whether they tend to stick with a particular brand or switch between brands.
    - **Product and service preferences:** What type of products or services they prefer, and why.
    - **Product and service usage:** How often they use the product or service and for what purpose.
    - **Online behavior:** What websites they visit, what social media platforms they use, what online applications they use regularly, do they produce online content or just consume, and how they interact with the content they consume (e.g., likes and comments).
    - **Decision-making process:** How they make purchasing decisions, whether they research products or services before buying, and what information they consider when making a decision.
    - **Motivations and pain points:** What motivates them to make a purchase, and what challenges and frustrations they face that your product or service can solve.

4. **Competition:** Understand who your competitors are and what they are offering.
5. **Market research:** Use surveys, focus groups, and other methods to gather data about your target market.

6. **Customer feedback:** Ask your best customers what they like most and least about your products and services, and what they wish you would start or stop doing.
7. **Analytics:** Analyze data from your website and other marketing channels to gain insights into your target market.
8. **Trends:** Stay up-to-date on industry trends and changes in consumer behavior to ensure your target market is still relevant and valuable.

===

It's important to regularly review and update your understanding of your target market as customer preferences and behaviors often change over time.

Defining Your Target Market Step-by-Step

Doing this for the first time can feel like a lot, so make it fun by breaking it down into small steps like the ones below. Use the suggested timelines to help you plan your schedule.

You may want to go back later and spend more time on certain steps. For now, though, it's important to get an initial overview of your target market without making this process overwhelming.

We realize some people geek out over research and data less than others, but this information is critically important and will become the foundation for the other chapters in this Guide.

NOTE: If you're one of those people who's not in love with research, here are some suggestions to make the time more enjoyable and pass by more quickly: Play some energizing music in the background (preferably without lyrics), give yourself a specific deadline for each step (set a timer), and reward yourself with some "play time" after each step.

STEP 1: Define your product or service (15 minutes)

Clearly define what you are selling. List each product and/or service separately, and then describe the features and benefits it provides to your customers.

STEP 2: Research the market (30 minutes)

We'll dive deeper into market research in Chapter 2. For now, spend 30 minutes doing some initial research to gain a better understanding of your industry, competitors, and potential customer base. To start, focus on conducting online research only.

STEP 3: Identify the demographics (15 minutes)

Use the data gathered from your research to identify the age, gender, income, education, and other quantifiable characteristics of your potential customers.

STEP 4: Determine psychographics (15 minutes)

Determine the values, beliefs, attitudes, interests, and lifestyles of your potential customers to better understand their motivations and behaviors.

STEP 5: Consider geographic location (10 minutes)

Determine the physical location of your potential customers and any regional differences in preferences and behaviors.

STEP 6: Analyze behavior patterns (30 minutes)

Analyze the purchasing behavior, product usage, and other behavioral patterns of your potential customers to understand their needs and wants.

STEP 7: Estimate the size and growth potential (20 minutes)

Estimate the size of the market and the potential for growth to identify opportunities for expansion and growth.

STEP 8: Segment the market (15 minutes)

Use the data gathered to segment the market into specific groups that share similar characteristics and behaviors.

STEP 9: Prioritize your market segments (10 minutes)

Determine which market segments offer the best potential for growth and profitability, based on factors such as size, growth potential, and competition.

===

Congratulations! You did it!

NOTE: We recommend you don't move forward in this Guide until you actually finish all 10 steps above.

The world is full of people who read books and DON'T take action. The fact that you've already gotten this far means that YOU are exceptional.

So if you haven't already, go back and finish each step. Make it FUN (using deadlines, breaks, and rewards) and you'll be done before you know it!

SPECIFIC SCENARIO: LiveLawn Landscaping Services

Larry Green, a fictional but passionate gardener, founded the imaginary "LiveLawn Landscaping Services" with a vision to provide top-notch lawn care to his local community.

In just over three years, his business flourished, growing from a one-man operation to a team of seven full-time lawn care professionals. Larry's hard work and dedication quickly earned him a reputation for excellent service, and word of mouth referrals poured in.

At first, this rapid growth seemed like a dream come true, but Larry's once-thriving business hit an invisible revenue ceiling over the past 12 months, leaving him puzzled and frustrated.

Eager to satisfy every customer, Larry took on jobs without considering location, property size, or profitability. His team traveled across town, servicing small residential lawns for $100 a month and large corporate office parks for several thousand dollars a month.

This unfocused approach stretched his team thin and left them unable to take on new clients. Although new referrals kept coming in, the potential profits from these customers weren't enough to justify hiring additional team members, and he had to turn down business.

The root of the problem was that Larry never defined his target market. His eagerness to please every potential customer led to an unsustainable business model.

Now, with a stalled business and an overworked team, Larry realizes that identifying a target market is crucial for streamlining his operations, serving his existing customers more efficiently, and preparing his business for future growth.

Here's how he defined his target market, according to the Step-by-Step process described in the previous section:

STEP 1: Define your product or service (15 minutes)

Larry spent 15 minutes clearly defining his lawn care services for both residential and commercial clients.

He listed the specific tasks his team performed, such as mowing, trimming, and seasonal maintenance, as well as any additional services, like landscape design and installation.

STEP 2: Research the market (30 minutes)

Larry looked at competitors, their offerings, and prices, and tried to identify any gaps or opportunities within the market for both residential and commercial clients.

STEP 3: Identify the demographics (15 minutes)

He identified the key demographic characteristics of his ideal residential clients, such as age, income level, and homeownership status.

Larry realized that his best residential clients were middle to upper-class homeowners with larger properties.

After reviewing his list of commercial clients, he realized his best corporate customers had well-maintained office parks or retail locations that required regular landscaping services.

STEP 4: Determine psychographics (15 minutes)

Larry identified that his ideal residential clients valued well-maintained lawns and landscapes, were environmentally conscious, and were willing to invest in professional services to maintain their properties.

For commercial clients, he found the best commercial property owners and managers prioritized curb appeal and a professional image.

STEP 5: Consider geographic location (10 minutes)

Larry thought hard about the geographic location of his ideal clients.

He decided to focus on clients within a 30-minute drive from his business, as this would reduce travel time and allow his team to service more clients efficiently.

STEP 6: Analyze behavior patterns (30 minutes)

After analyzing the behavior patterns of his clients, such as their preferred communication methods, frequency of service, and willingness to refer others, Larry discovered that the clients who were more engaged with his team and communicated their needs clearly were more likely to be satisfied and refer new clients.

STEP 7: Estimate the size and growth potential (20 minutes)

When he looked closely at his company's income over the past three years, Larry realized that focusing on larger residential properties and commercial clients offered more revenues and a higher potential to scale his business.

STEP 8: Segment the market (15 minutes)

Larry segmented his target market into two primary groups: residential clients with larger properties and commercial clients with office parks or retail locations.

This allowed him to tailor his marketing efforts and service offerings to each segment more effectively.

STEP 9: Prioritize your market segments (10 minutes)

Finally, Larry decided to focus primarily on acquiring commercial clients since they had bigger budgets, and the additional revenues would give him the ability to grow his team and his company.

As a secondary focus, he would occasionally take on larger residential properties, especially if they belonged to employees of his corporate clients. This strategy would allow him to maximize his resources and continue to expand his business effectively.

===

After defining his target market, Larry experienced several positive results that transformed his business.

By focusing on commercial clients and larger residential properties, he was able to increase efficiency, maximize the use of his team's skills, and boost revenues.

The additional income allowed him to expand his team and accommodate new clients without overextending his resources.

Larry also noticed an improvement in client satisfaction as he tailored his services more effectively to their needs.

Ultimately, this strategic approach to defining his target market helped Larry break through the revenue ceiling, streamline his operations, and set LiveLawn Landscaping Services on a path to sustainable growth.

Strategy Snapshot For Defining Your Target Market

Identifying a target market is crucial for any business looking to succeed.

To identify your target market, you need to follow a step-by-step process that involves

- Defining your product or service
- Researching the market
- Identifying demographics
- Identifying psychographics
- Considering geographic location
- Analyzing behavior patterns
- Estimating the size and growth potential
- Segmenting the market, and
- Prioritizing segments

By following this process, you'll gain a better understanding of your dream customers and create more relevant and effective marketing messages that will help you stand out from your competitors.

Remember to stay focused on your target market, as this will help you tailor your product or service to meet their needs and increase your probability of success.

Take The First Step

Congratulations on making it through the first chapter!

As mentioned in the "How To Use This Guide" section earlier, the only way you're going to grow your small business is by TAKING ACTION on what you've learned.

Before reading any further, here's what we suggest you do next:

Schedule an hour on your calendar to conduct market research by reviewing industry reports and websites, analyzing local competition, and gathering insights from existing customers.

This will help you gain a better understanding of the needs and wants of your potential customers and allow you to create a more relevant and effective marketing strategy.

By taking this step, you will be better equipped to tailor your product or service to meet the needs of your target market and stand out from your competitors.

===

NOTE: If you've already done this, or if there's something else you learned in this chapter that you feel takes a higher priority, then go with your gut.

The bottom line is that "book smarts" is not enough; you have to APPLY what you've learned in order to get on the path to rapid business growth.

Once you've taken action on defining your target market, you can move on to the next chapter, or if you prefer, skip ahead the chapter that speaks to you the loudest.

You are on your way to creating the business you've always dreamed about!

Chapter 2:
How Conducting Market Research Helps You Create Products And Services Customers Want

*"Research is formalized curiosity.
It is poking and prying with a purpose."*

— Zora Neale Hurston

Why Is Conducting Market Research Important?

Having identified your target market, which pinpoints your ideal customers, it's time to delve into market research to understand the market's size, trends, growth potential, and competitive landscape.

This exploration will guide you in determining the most suitable products, services, pricing, and overall business strategies tailored specifically for your market.

In other words, market research focuses more on the "what" aspects rather than the "who" of your target market.

When it comes to running your small business, conducting market research is a crucial step to success for multiple reasons:

1. **It helps you understand your customers better.**
   It lets you know what they like, what they don't like, and what they need. By gathering this information, you'll be able to create products and services that meet their needs and preferences, which ultimately means more sales for your business.

2. **It also helps you understand your competition.**
   Find out what they're doing well and what they're not doing so well. This information will help you make informed decisions about how to differentiate your business and stand out in a crowded market.

3. **It saves you time and money.**
   By knowing what your customers want and need, you'll avoid wasting time and resources creating and marketing products and services that won't sell.

4. **It makes your marketing more efficient.**
   When doing your research, you'll identify the most effective and efficient ways to target potential customers, thereby reducing your marketing expenses.

5. **You'll make better business decisions.**
   Your choices will be based on data and insights rather than guesswork, which increases your likelihood of success.

"What Happens If I Don't Conduct Market Research?"

If you don't do your homework before going out to sell your products and services to the world, here are a few issues you might run into:

- **Poor pricing strategies**
  Market research will help determine the optimal price point for your products or services. Without this information, you'll probably set your prices too high or too low, which can negatively impact your revenue and profitability.

- **Negative customer feedback**
  If you don't understand your customers' needs and preferences, you'll end up providing products and services that don't meet their expectations. This will result in negative customer feedback, which can harm your business's reputation.

- **Inability to forecast sales**
  Market research provides insights into consumer demand and buying patterns, which are essential for accurate sales forecasting. Without this information, it is difficult to anticipate sales trends and adjust production or staffing levels accordingly.

- **Difficulty securing funding**
  Investors and lenders often want to see evidence that a business has conducted market research to support its growth plans. Without this information, it will be difficult to secure the funding you need to expand your business.

- **Higher risk of failure**
  Market research helps you identify potential obstacles and mitigate risks. Without this information, your business will be more vulnerable to failure, especially in the early stages of your journey.

===

As you can see, market research is a crucial step for any business looking to succeed.

Thorough and ongoing market research provides you with valuable insights, help you refine your strategies, and keep you ahead of the competition. It sets your business up for long-term success and growth.

The Essential Elements Of Conducting Market Research

If you want to conduct effective market research for your small business, there are a few key elements you should include.

Here are the most important:

1. **Identify your research goals**
   Before you start, it's important to know what you want to achieve with your research. What questions do you want to answer? What do you hope to learn? For example, "What are the top three factors that influence our target market's decision-making process when choosing a product or service similar to ours?" Setting clear research goals will help guide your efforts and ensure you gather the information you need.

2. **Determine your target market**
   Who do you want to study? Who are your customers, and who are your potential customers? By defining your target market, you'll make sure you're collecting information that's relevant and useful to your business. (You should have done this already in Chapter 1, but if not, go back and identify your target market now so you have it crystal clear in your mind going forward.)

3. **Choose your research methods**
   There are lots of different ways to gather data, from surveys to focus groups to online research. Pick the methods that make the most sense for your business, your budget, and your goals.

4. **Collect your data**
   Once you know what you want to learn and how you plan to learn it, it's time to start collecting your data. Make sure you're getting a diverse range of opinions from your target market and that your sample size is large enough to be statistically significant.

5. **Analyze your results**
   Once you've collected your data, it's time to make sense of it. Look for patterns and trends, and use your findings to inform your business decisions.

6. **Keep an eye on your budget**
   Conducting market research can be expensive, but it doesn't have to be. Keep an eye on your budget and choose methods that fit within your means. There are many affordable options, like online surveys or social media polls, that can provide valuable insights.

7. **Stay up-to-date**
   Markets are constantly changing, so it's important to stay up-to-date with the latest trends, technology, and industry developments. By keeping your finger on the pulse of your market, you'll make more informed decisions and stay ahead of your competition.

By following these essential elements, you'll be able to conduct market research that gives you valuable insights into your customers, your competitors, and your industry.

Conducting Market Research Step-by-Step

Just like before, make it fun by breaking your market research down into small steps.

Play some energizing music in the background (preferably without lyrics so you can hear yourself think), give yourself a specific deadline for each step (set a timer), and reward yourself with a healthy snack or some "play time" after each step.

STEP 1: Create a focused list of questions (30 minutes)

While it's tempting to ask a lot of questions up front, it's better to start with a smaller set of the most important questions to avoid overwhelming people.

Consider limiting your list to around 10-15 questions that are most relevant to the topics you want to explore. This will guide your efforts and help you avoid overwhelming your audience with too many questions.

STEP 2: Create a profile of your target market (3 hours)

If you haven't already done this back in Chapter 1, go back for detailed instructions on how to do this **right now**.

You'll need to know their demographic information, needs, preferences, and more to better understand who is most likely to buy from you and what information is most important to collect.

STEP 3: Make a budget (10 minutes)

Decide how much you're willing to spend to get your initial market research.

Unless you're hiring other people to help you, or you are doing this for a multi-million-dollar company, this whole process shouldn't be expensive.

Consider using free or low-cost research methods, such as online surveys, to save money.

STEP 4: Go get answers to your questions (1 week)

Collect data using the list of questions you came up with in Step 1. Collect enough information to get a representative sample and make sure the data is accurate and reliable.

Asking people face-to-face is ideal, but if you're the shy type, post your questions on social media or email them to your target market.

Many people won't be able to drop everything to answer you immediately, so give them a few days. Then follow up if necessary.

You might even consider giving people an incentive to helping you complete your survey. For example, a small freebie or a 10% discount on one of your products or services.

STEP 5: Analyze your data and draw conclusions (1-3 hours)

Organize your data and look for patterns and trends to identify insights and draw meaningful conclusions from your research.

STEP 6: Stay up-to-date (2-3 hours/month)

Stay current on market trends, consumer behaviors, and emerging technologies that may impact your business.

Keep up-to-date by attending industry events, reading publications, and following social media accounts of thought leaders in your industry.

STEP 7: Sell something (1 month)

The REAL market research is done when people pay YOU. Based on your market research, offer something for sale. Get feedback on your offer regarding the price and the benefits.

The value should be multiple times higher than your asking price. For example, if your cost is $100, show how the value to the customer is at least $300 or more (preferably a LOT more).

If the real or perceived value is not high enough, ask your target market for help to make your offer even better. Keep iterating until someone pays you cold, hard cash for your product or service.

For example, when Zappos (the online shoe company) started selling shoes online, *they sold shoes they didn't have yet.*

First they sold the shoes, *then* they fulfilled the orders by buying the shoes at full retail price at local shoe stores, which they subsequently shipped to their online customers — just to prove the market existed for online shoe sales. (source: https://hbr.org/2010/05/how-zappos-was-born-place-bets)

SPECIFIC SCENARIO: Transcendental T-Shirts

Transcendental T-Shirts, a fictitious company with a fictitious founder by the name of Rainbow Summers, specializes in selling unique T-shirts with spiritual and philosophical themes.

Here's how Ms. Summers might conduct her market research using the step-by-step checklist:

STEP 1: Create a focused list of questions (30 minutes)

Rainbow starts off by creating a list of 15 questions, including:

- What kind of spiritual or philosophical themes would you like to see on a T-shirt?
- How important is sustainability to you when purchasing clothing?
- Would you be interested in purchasing a subscription box of T-shirts with new designs each month?
- What size T-shirt do you wear?
- Do you prefer 100% cotton, a cotton/polyester blend, or 100% polyester?
- ...and so on

STEP 2: Create a profile of your target market (4 hours)

Rainbow and her team already know that their target market is people interested in spiritual and philosophical themes, so they use their existing knowledge to create a more detailed profile, including age range (25-45), income level ($30,000+), and social media preferences (active on Instagram and Facebook).

STEP 3: Make a budget (10 minutes)

Rainbow decides to use free and low-cost research methods for their market research, including online surveys and social media polls. She sets a budget of $100 to cover any incidental expenses.

STEP 4: Go get answers to your questions (1 week)

She sends out her 15-question survey to the company's email list and posts it on their social media channels.

Because she knows how valuable voice-of-customer is for future growth, Rainbow offers a 20% discount to anyone who completes the survey on their next online purchase.

STEP 5: Analyze your data and draw conclusions (1-3 hours)

The team receives over 500 responses to their survey within a week, which they analyze for patterns and trends using a spreadsheet.

They find that customers are most interested in T-shirts with themes related to mindfulness and environmental sustainability.

They also see a high level of interest in a subscription box service.

STEP 6: Stay up-to-date (2-3 hours/month)

Rainbow follows the social media accounts of thought leaders in her industry, attends local events related to spirituality and sustainability, and reads industry publications to stay up-to-date on emerging trends and changes in their market.

STEP 7: Sell something (1 month)

The team at Transcendental T-Shirts starts offering a new line of T-shirts with themes related to mindfulness and sustainability.

In addition, they unveil a brand-new subscription box service. The new offers are featured prominently on their website and receive both positive and negative feedback from their customers.

They use the feedback to make improvements to their products and continue to iterate until both new product lines are profitable.

===

By doing their market research, Rainbow and her team at Transcendental T-Shirts create demand in advance for their products and avoid wasting time, energy, and expense by NOT assuming what their customers and prospects want.

Strategy Snapshot For Conducting Market Research

Market research is a crucial aspect of any business as it helps companies to understand their customers, their competitors, and the market in which they operate.

It involves the collection and analysis of data to provide insights that guide business decisions.

Effective market research starts with a well-defined problem or question that the research seeks to answer.

To conduct market research, businesses should create a focused list of questions, create a profile of their target market, make a budget, collect data, analyze the data, and stay on top of changes in the market.

The goal is to identify patterns, trends, and insights that will inform the development of products, services, marketing strategies, and more.

It's important to keep in mind that market research is an ongoing process, as markets, customers, and trends are constantly evolving.

Take The First Step

If you have not yet conducted market research for your business, the most important thing you can do is take the time to create a focused list of questions that are most relevant to the topics you want to explore.

Limit your list to around 10-15 questions to guide your efforts and avoid overwhelming your audience with too many questions.

By doing this, you will have a better understanding of your target market, competitors, and industry trends, and make data-driven decisions to improve your business.

Take some time right now to create a list of focused questions and start your market research journey today!

Chapter 3:
How Developing Your Brand Identity Helps You Increase Customer Loyalty And Eliminate The Competition

"Your brand is what people say about you when you are not in the room."

— Jeff Bezos

Why Is Developing Your Brand Identity Important?

Your brand identity is the way that your customers perceive and remember their interactions with your company, products, and services.

It's also the way they talk about you to their family, friends, and social media followers.

Brand identity applies to all of the following: a company, a product, a service, or a person.

Essentially, anything that can be recognized by a specific name or symbol and has a unique set of values, personality, and characteristics can have a brand identity.

A person's brand identity is focused on their personal characteristics, values, and reputation. It includes their name, image, and messaging that communicates who they are, what they stand for, and how they can add value to their audience.

A company's brand identity reflects its values, mission, and culture. It encompasses everything from the company's name, logo, and visual identity, to the way it communicates with its customers, employees, and stakeholders.

A product's brand identity is focused on its unique features and benefits that differentiate the product from all others. It includes the product's name, packaging, logo, and messaging that communicates its value proposition to the target audience.

A service's brand identity is centered around the experience the service provides to customers. It includes the company's name, logo, and visual identity, as well as the tone and style of its communication and the quality of its customer service.

===

We'll be focusing on your company's brand identity in this chapter. For personalized help on the other types of brand identity mentioned above, contact us via our website at www.RapidBusinessGrowth.co.

There are many reasons why you need to start developing your brand identity right away.

Here are 5 good ones:

1. **Stand out from the competition**
   Developing a unique visual and messaging style helps your small business differentiate itself from competitors and makes it easier for customers to recognize and remember your company.

2. **Increase customer loyalty**
   A strong brand identity builds an emotional connection with your customers and makes them more likely to keep coming back.

3. **Heighten brand recognition**
   Consistently using your business's visual and messaging style across all channels heightens brand recognition and makes your small business more memorable to prospects and customers.

4. **Bolster rapid business growth**
   A well-designed brand identity creates a foundation for attracting new customers, partners, vendors, and potential investors.

5. **Attract top talent**
   Creating a clear and compelling brand identity that reflects the values and culture of your small business attracts top talent.

"What Happens If I Don't Develop A Brand Identity?"

Without a clear and consistent brand identity, your small business will likely face a range of challenges that can impact your growth and success.

Here's a few to look out for:

- **Difficulty standing out**
  Without a distinctive and consistent way to represent your business, it's difficult to stand out. You get lost in the crowd, and even current customers have a hard time remembering you.

- **Awkward messaging**
  If you don't have a defined way of communicating your values, mission, and unique selling proposition, you end up with a bunch of different messages that don't fit together. Your messaging sounds awkward and confuses customers.

- **Weak customer loyalty**
  If your brand identity is not engaging, it's hard to build an emotional connection with your customers and prospects. They feel like they don't know your business very well, which makes it easier for them to go to a competitor.

- **Inability to attract top talent**
  If you can't clearly convey your values and culture, it's tough to attract the best employees to your business. They can't figure out what your business is all about, and that makes them less interested in working for you.

- **Poor customer experience**
  If you don't have a consistent way of providing an enjoyable experience for your customers, it's tough to delight them and keep them happy as customers. They don't know what to expect from your business, which leads to negative reviews, bad word-of-mouth, and lost sales.

===

This is why developing a brand identity is crucial for your small business. It helps establish credibility, increase customer recognition, and create robust relationships with customers and employees alike.

The Essential Elements Of Developing Your Brand Identity

Here are 10 essential elements to consider when developing your brand identity, each of which plays a vital role in establishing your small business's unique identity and message.

1. **Brand strategy**
   A clear and concise plan that outlines your business goals, target audience, and brand message.

2. **Brand purpose**
   The underlying reason why your business exists and the values that drive it.

3. **Brand positioning**
   The unique place that your business occupies in the marketplace, and how it compares to competitors.

4. **Brand voice**
   The tone, language, and personality that your small business uses to communicate with customers.

5. **Brand name**
   The name of your business that sets the tone and establishes an identity for your brand.

6. **Brand logo**
   A visual representation of your brand, which should be distinctive, memorable, and easily recognizable.

7. **Brand color palette**
   A selection of colors that represent your brand and evoke certain emotions or associations.

8. **Brand typography**
   The typeface and font that you use in your branding materials, which can affect how your brand is perceived.

9. **Brand imagery**
   The visual elements such as graphics, illustrations, and photographs that you use to represent your brand, which should align with your brand voice and personality.

10. **Brand guidelines**
    A set of rules and standards that define how your brand should be used across all channels and touchpoints. These guidelines ensure that your brand is consistent and cohesive, and helps to build recognition and trust with customers.

Developing Your Brand Identity Step-by-Step

To drive rapid growth for your small business, it's important to develop a strong brand identity that stands out and resonates with your customers.

Follow these steps to develop a unique and consistent brand identity that represents your business and builds trust with your customers.

=====

NOTE: We realize you have likely already gone through some or all of this process for your small business. For instance, your business probably has a name and logo already.

But maybe you didn't put the same thought into your brand identity that you would if you had known what you know now.

If you already have a strong brand identity, stick with it, of course.

If not, or if it's not fully fleshed out yet, give yourself permission to recreate your brand identity with a stronger, simpler, more memorable one.

=====

STEP 1: Establish your brand purpose (1 hour)

Start by defining the values that drive your business, and create a statement that explains why your business exists and what it stands for. Think about what makes your business unique and why you want to do what you do.

STEP 2: Position your brand (3 hours)

Think about what led you to start your business, what makes it unique, and what values drive your business. Develop a narrative that tells your story and connects with your target audience.

STEP 3: Develop your brand voice (1 day)

Determine the tone of voice that best represents your brand. Do you want it to be humorous, professional, sarcastic, or serious? Is it geared towards 5-year-olds or 55-year-olds (or somewhere in-between)?

Once you've written down a description of your brand voice, review your website home page to check whether that tone of voice is used on your site.

STEP 4: Choose your brand name (3 hours)

Pick a name that is easy to remember, easy to pronounce, aligns with your brand purpose and personality, and has an available Internet domain to go with it.

This is the name that your customers will associate with your business, so choose wisely!

STEP 5: Choose your brand color palette (2 hours)

Select 2-3 primary colors (and optionally 1-2 secondary colors) that align with your brand personality and that evoke the desired emotions and associations.

STEP 6: Create your brand logo (2 weeks)

Create a visual representation of your brand that is unique, memorable, and recognizable. Your logo should communicate your brand purpose and personality. Think about the colors, shapes, and symbols that best represent your brand.

Then hire a professional graphic designer to create your logo. You can find freelancers on Upwork or Fiverr that can create unique, professional logos for $200 or less. (Avoid logo templates that are used by hundreds of other companies.)

STEP 7: Choose your brand typography (2 weeks, concurrent with logo)

Choose a typeface that reflects your brand personality and tone of voice. The right font can make a big difference in how people perceive your brand.

STEP 8: Choose your brand imagery (1 week)

Review the brand imagery on your website's home page. Does it align with your brand identity? If not, find some initial graphics, illustrations, and/or photographs that align with your brand purpose and personality.

These should communicate the desired emotions and associations that you want your customers to feel when they think of your brand. Have your web designer incorporate the new imagery on your home page.

STEP 9: Create a basic logo usage guide (2 hours)

Establish guidelines on how your logo should be used, including placement, size, typography, and color variations. This will help ensure that your logo is used consistently across all touchpoints.

SPECIFIC SCENARIO: The Suds-O-Rific Soap Company

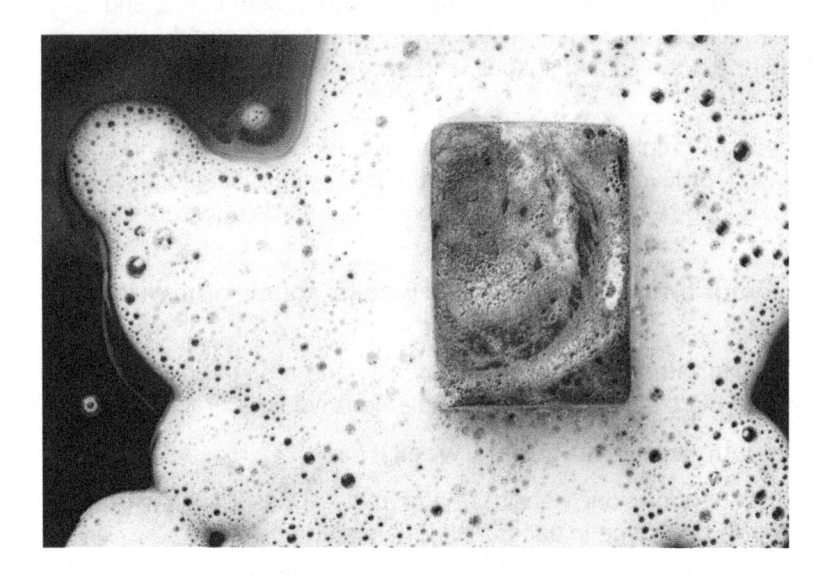

The imaginary "Suds-O-Rific Soap" is a small business that sells soap, shampoo, bath bombs, and other personal care items.

They currently have a bland and boring image in the market. But in reality, the husband and wife founders are fun, adventurous people who love to compete in mud runs at least once a month.

When they first started competing in mud run races, they had a hard time washing off all the dirt and mud (and who knows what else) that accumulated during each race.

So they created their own special exfoliating soap products to make themselves feel extra fresh and clean after every race.

When they shared their soaps, shampoos, and bath bombs with family and friends, word-of-mouth took off and they turned their soap-making hobby into an actual business.

But they didn't know anything about developing a brand identity, and so to the outside world, they were just another soap company.

To help bring their unique personality and values to the forefront, they decided to develop a brand identity for their company.

Here's how they did it, following the step-by-step checklist.

STEP 1: Establish your brand purpose (1 hour)

The founders of Suds-O-Rific Soap, being avid mud runners themselves, know what it feels like to want a soap product that can truly clean the body after a mud run and other outdoor adventures.

They create the following brand purpose statement:

"For the mud runners, hikers, and outdoor enthusiasts, our soap is your partner in grime. Tough enough to tackle any adventure, and gentle enough to leave your skin feeling soft and refreshed."

STEP 2: Position your brand (3 hours)

The founders want to position themselves as a fun, adventurous, and effective alternative to traditional soap products.

They decide to develop a brand narrative that highlights their own personal experiences as mud runners, and how they invented exfoliating soaps that thoroughly clean your body after an outdoor adventure.

They want to be the soap of first choice for mud runners, hikers, and outdoor enthusiasts who want personal care products as fun and exciting as their hobbies.

STEP 3: Develop your brand voice (1 day)

To develop their brand voice, the founders decide to go with fun and humorous tone of voice that reflects their own personalities. They want to keep it light-hearted and fun.

With the help of ChatGPT, they rewrote the copy on their homepage to ensure that their message is delivered with the tone of voice consistent with their brand.

STEP 4: Choose your brand name (3 hours)

They decide to change their company name from "Suds-O-Rific Soap" to a new name that better reflects their brand purpose and personality: "Sudsy Mudsy Soap Co."

They choose this name because it is memorable, easy to pronounce, evokes the outdoors, and aligns well with their exfoliating soaps that get people really, really, really clean.

STEP 5: Choose your brand color palette (2 hours)

To reflect the new name, the founders select a primary color palette that includes an earthy brown to evoke mud and dirt, along with a bright blue to conjure thoughts of water and cleanliness.

They also incorporate a secondary color palette of muted earth tones to emphasize the natural ingredients used in their soap products.

STEP 6: Create your brand logo (2 weeks)

To create their new logo, the founders of the newly renamed "Sudsy Mudsy Soap Co." work with a professional graphic designer to create a unique and memorable logo that reflects their brand purpose and personality.

The finished logo incorporates a mud-colored soap bar surrounded by bright blue soap bubbles to show the how getting really dirty is intertwined with getting really clean.

STEP 7: Choose your brand typography (2 weeks, concurrent with logo)

The graphic designer works with the founders to choose a playful, hand-drawn typeface that reflects their brand personality and tone of voice. The font is legible and easy to read while also conveying a sense of fun.

STEP 8: Choose your brand imagery (1 week)

After reviewing the imagery on their website's homepage, the founders decide to showcase the joy and fulfillment that comes from embracing life's messy moments and emerging fresh and renewed.

So they replace the images on their site with before and after photos of themselves during mud runs (before) and dressed casually after getting clean (after), as well as before and after photos of friends who are fellow mud runners and outdoor enthusiasts.

STEP 9: Create a logo usage guide (4 hours)

They establish guidelines for how their logo should be used, specifying a minimum size so the logo is always legible, color variations allowed, and examples of how the logo should be displayed in differing promotional materials and online.

They also disallowed the distortion and/or stretching of the logo and changing any part of it.

===

In the end, the founders of the (still imaginary) Sudsy Mudsy Soap Co. had a clear brand purpose that represented their fun and sarcastic personalities.

By positioning their brand as directly serving outdoor enthusiasts, they were able to connect with customers who were looking for unique, playful soap products.

Their brand voice, color palette, typography, and imagery all worked together to create a cohesive brand identity.

By following the step-by-step checklist, they were able to create a brand that truly represented who they were as a business.

Now, Sudsy Mudsy Soap Co. stands out in the crowded soap market, with a brand that reflects their values and resonates with their customers.

Strategy Snapshot For Developing Your Brand Identity

Developing a brand identity is an essential part of building a business.

It helps you to establish what your business stands for and creates a unique identity for your company that sets it apart from the competition.

To develop your brand identity, you need to first define your business's purpose, values, and personality.

This involves thinking about what makes your business unique and what led you to start it.

Once you have established your purpose, you need to position your brand, think about your target audience, and develop a brand voice that reflects your personality and values.

Choosing a name that aligns with your brand and creating a unique, recognizable logo is also crucial, as is selecting the right color palette and typography.

Finally, create a logo usage guide to ensure consistency across all touchpoints.

By following these steps, you can establish a strong brand identity that will help your business to grow and succeed.

Take The First Step

The one most important thing you can do today to create progress in developing your brand identity is to establish your brand purpose.

Spend an hour thinking about the values that drive your business, what makes it unique, and why you want to do what you do.

Create a statement that explains why your business exists and what it stands for.

This will help you define your brand's direction and will serve as the foundation for all other branding decisions.

Start by asking yourself, "why did I start my business?" and let that guide you.

Chapter 4:
How Setting Marketing Goals And Objectives Can Skyrocket Sales

"Unless you have definite, precise, clearly set goals, you are not going to realize the maximum potential that lies within you."

— Zig Ziglar

Why Is Setting Marketing Goals And Objectives Important?

"Marketing goals and objectives" and a "marketing plan" are related concepts, but they are not the same thing.

A marketing plan is a comprehensive document that outlines your company's roadmap for achieving goals over a long period, typically a year or more.

Marketing goals and objectives are short-term outcomes, typically weekly or monthly, that businesses measure to track their progress against their long-term marketing plan.

In other words, marketing goals and objectives help you and your team stay focused and motivated on a daily basis on your way to achieving your long-term plans.

Here are 7 reasons why setting short-term marketing goals and objectives is so important:

1. **They're easy to communicate.**
   Short-term marketing goals are easy to communicate to your team, making sure everyone is on the same page and working towards the same objectives.

2. **You get quick results.**
   You'll often see the results right away (in a week or a month) rather than waiting for three months or longer. Near-instant feedback will be very motivating for you and your team.

3. **They're easier to adjust.**
   If something isn't working in the short term, you'll be able to quickly pivot and try a different approach.

4. **Stay focused.**
   Is it easier to concentrate on your *annual* fitness plan...? Or how you're going to eat and move your body *today*? We tend to have short attention spans and a desire for instant gratification. Short-term goals make it harder to get distracted.

5. **They maximize your efficiency.**
   By breaking down your long-term marketing plan into small chunks and steps, you'll have a better sense of which tasks will have the most impact, so you can focus your time and energy more effectively.

6. **Improve your cash flow.**
   Cash flow is king. You need enough money coming in each week to pay your bills, pay your team, grow your business, and stay solvent. Short term goals make sure you're measuring revenues over days and weeks rather than months.

7. **Helps you build momentum.**
   The ability to identify your wins and obstacles quickly is important. It

builds excitement for your team, which helps you achieve even bigger goals over time.

"What Happens If I Don't Set Marketing Goals And Objectives?"

Failing to set short-term marketing goals and objectives can have significant negative consequences for your business.

Here are a few you should be aware of:

- **Missed opportunities**
  Short-term goals let you take advantage of unexpected opportunities, which will pass you by if you don't move quickly.

- **Ineffective marketing**
  If you're not checking your results frequently, you'll keep doing things that aren't working, which then leads to...

- **Wasted resources**
  For every day your marketing isn't driving results, you're wasting time and money.

- **Low productivity**
  If your marketing team isn't analyzing the data and improving your messaging and funnels on the regular, they're not using their time as effectively as they could be.

- **Cash crunches**
  Without short-term goals and objectives, your business will struggle to generate consistent revenue, leading to cash flow problems.

- **Limited growth**
  Your business will struggle to grow in a competitive market, capping your potential success.

===

By setting specific goals and objectives that cover short periods of time, your business will stay on track, adjust to changes quickly, and achieve the long-term goals set out in your marketing plan.

The Essential Elements Of Setting Marketing Goals And Objectives

To make sure your short-term marketing goals are effective, they need to include the following elements:

1. **Specificity**
   When you prepare to go on a trip and say the destination is "10 miles from here," it's easier to measure than the vague term "far away." Similarly, your marketing goals and objectives need to be specific and measurable so you can track your progress every step of the way.

2. **Time-bound**
   The best goals have deadlines. Otherwise, you could easily take a month to accomplish something that can be done in a few days (a phenomenon known as "Parkinson's Law").

3. **Reality-based**
   They should be attainable and realistic, and take into account your resources, capabilities, and constraints.

4. **Clearly communicated**
   If you don't clearly communicate your short-term marketing goals and objectives to your team, how can they possibly help you achieve them?

5. **Collaborative**
   When your team is involved in choosing your goals and objectives, they feel more invested in them and are more motivated to work hard to achieve them.

6. **Prioritized**
   Not every goal is equally important. Prioritize them based on their impact to your business, the time it will take to achieve them, and the resources you will need.

7. **Data-driven**
   Your goals and objectives should be informed by data and insights about the current market, your target audience, and your competition.

8. **Actionable**
   Many times, the goals we set are too broad and can be interpreted and accomplished in multiple ways (some of which are more efficient and cost-effective than others). Break each goal down into actionable steps, so your team knows exactly what needs to be done.

9. **Re-evaluated regularly**
   Your goals and objectives should be evaluated regularly to assess progress and make adjustments as needed.

Setting Marketing Goals And Objectives Step-by-Step

Here's an example of a badly formed marketing goal: "I want to sell more widgets."

Let's improve this goal, step by step, using the 9 Essential Elements of setting marketing goals and objectives:

STEP 1: Specificity

Instead of the vague goal of "selling more widgets", let's make it more specific. For example, "I want to sell 100 widgets".

STEP 2: Time-bound

Our goal needs to have a deadline. Let's give ourselves one week (5 business days) to sell 100 widgets.

STEP 3: Reality-based

It's important to make sure the goal is realistic and attainable. If you usually sell 10 widgets a week, setting a goal of selling 100 widgets in one week may not be realistic. With that in mind, let's adjust the goal to something that's aggressive but achievable, such as selling 15 widgets in one week.

STEP 4: Clearly communicated

If you keep your goal a secret, how can your team help you achieve it? Everyone involved in the process of selling widgets should be on the same page. Call an "all hands" meeting with your team and let them know about your goal to sell 15 widgets in the next 5 days.

STEP 5: Collaborative

Collaboration is an essential factor to achieving your goals, especially for stretch goals like this one. Ask your team to brainstorm 10 different ways your company can sell 15 widgets in 5 days.

STEP 6: Prioritized

What else is your team working on this week? Should they drop everything else to make sure they hit your goal? Make sure your sales goal fits in with everything else going on this week.

STEP 7: Data-driven

It's important to use data to inform your goals. Look at sales figures from the past to see how you accomplished them and what changes you'd need to make to reach your goal.

Maybe you have two salespeople on your team and they each sell 5 widgets a week. Based on that data, you decide you need to hire a third salesperson to reach your goal. Unfortunately, you realize that's not realistic because hiring the right person usually takes time.

Instead, you are reminded of a special sales promotion you held last quarter that resulted in 17 widgets being sold in a single week. If you did it once, you can do it again, right? Dive into the details of that promotion so you can reproduce the sale.

STEP 8: Actionable

Your goal needs to be broken down into actionable steps. For example, find out what was involved with the sales promotion last quarter, and reproduce the sale step-by-step, starting with choosing the target market, creating a modified version of the marketing copy, updating your website and social media pages, etc.

STEP 9: Re-evaluated regularly

Regularly evaluate your progress and adjust your plan if needed. Since your goal is to sell 15 widgets in 5 business days, that's an average of 3 widgets a day.

Check in with your team daily throughout the week to make sure your sales goal of 3 widgets a day is on track, and if not, make the necessary changes to your marketing and sales efforts.

===

By following the Essential Elements, we were able to turn a weak goal into a strong one.

We started with a broad, vague, and badly formed goal without a deadline.

We transformed it into a specific, realistic, time-bound, and actionable goal that can be achieved in one week with the help of a collaborative team effort.

That's the power of effective goal-setting and teamwork in action.

SPECIFIC SCENARIO: RejuvaFusion Wellness

The completely made-up company, RejuvaFusion Wellness, is excited to announce the launch of their new product, "Vitamin W".

To spread the word and make sure everyone knows about their amazing new supplement, they need to create a single web page that highlights all of the benefits and features of Vitamin W, along with a way to order it online.

Here is an example of how they take this short-term goal (create a single web page for a new product) and break it down using the essential elements of setting marketing goals and objectives:

Monday

- <u>Set a deadline</u>
  Based on the available resources, including web designers, copywriters, coders, and a sufficient budget, RejuvaFusion decides that this single web page can be up and running by the end of the week (i.e., within 5 business days).

- <u>Establish a clear and specific goal</u>
  They decide the page will inform potential customers about the benefits and features of Vitamin W, and include a way to immediately purchase the product online.

- <u>Gather data</u>
  Having sold supplements to thousands of customers over the past five years, RejuvaFusion gathers data based on past sales as well as current trends in the supplement industry, including confirming their target

market profile is up-to-date (*see Chapter 1: Defining Your Target Market*). They use all this information to develop content that speaks directly to their current and potential customers.

- Collaborate with the team
  They bring the entire team together to brainstorm ideas and identify key features of the web page. They also discuss potential obstacles that might come up during the week and how to overcome them.

Tuesday

- Prioritize the most important elements
  Based on their research and collaboration with the team, RejuvaFusion decides which elements need to be on the web page, and which should be left off. They agree that the page needs to contain recent images of the product, information about known and potential health benefits, customer testimonials (from their initial tests), a call-to-action, and an order form.

- Develop a plan
  RejuvaFusion creates a plan for how they will structure the content and design of the web page, how they will communicate their new product through email and social media, how to respond to questions, and the fulfillment process. They also discuss what to do if sales are dramatically higher or lower than expected.

Wednesday

- Develop the content
  The team uses the plan developed on Tuesday to create content for the web page, including sales copy, product images, a short video, a few experts talking about the benefits of Vitamin W, and customer testimonials.

- Choose a design
  They choose a design that is working well for one of their other supplements, and apply it to the new page.

Thursday

- Test the page
  The team tests the new page to ensure it meets RejuvaFusion's standards for functionality, speed, and usability. They make the necessary adjustments to the design and content based on feedback.

- Gather Feedback
  Everyone on the team reviews the page to test the functionality, give feedback on the page elements (copy, images, video, etc.) and make the necessary changes to improve the page. They also contact a few of their best customers for a "sneak preview" and offer them a discount in return for their honest feedback.

Friday

- <u>Launch the web page</u>
  Once the RejuvaFusion team has completed the page and is satisfied with the content and design, they launch the web page and tell all their customers and followers about it.

- <u>Optimize the page</u>
  It's not over yet. Once real traffic starts coming in, they regularly re-evaluate the page's performance and conversion rates and make multiple improvements.

===

By following these steps, RejuvaFusion Wellness created a web page for their new (and fictional) product, Vitamin W, in one week.

They took into account the essential elements of setting short-term marketing goals and objectives, including being specific, reality-based, time-bound, clearly communicated, prioritized, data-driven, actionable, collaborative, and re-evaluated regularly.

Strategy Snapshot For Setting Marketing Goals And Objectives

Setting marketing goals and objectives is a crucial step for any business looking to grow and succeed.

Short-term goals provide focus and momentum for your team, allowing for quick adjustments and adaptability in a rapidly changing market.

It's important that your goals are specific, time-bound, reality-based, clearly communicated, collaborative, prioritized, data-driven, actionable, and regularly re-evaluated.

Start with your marketing plan (*see Chapter 3: Developing a Marketing Plan*) and break your long-term goals down into short-term goals and objectives.

Prioritize your goals based on their impact and consider your resources, capabilities, and constraints.

Use data and insights to inform your decisions and collaborate with your team to build buy-in and motivation.

Finally, regularly re-evaluate your progress to ensure you are on track and make adjustments as needed.

Setting short-term goals will help you stay focused and achieve quick results, which can be a powerful motivator for you and your team.

Ultimately, short-term marketing goals and objectives provide the foundation for long-term growth and success in the competitive world of small business.

Take The First Step

If you want to make progress in your business, the most important thing you can do right now is to identify the top priority goal in your annual marketing plan.

Look at your plan and determine what the single most important thing is that you need to achieve this year.

Once you have identified that goal, break it down into three smaller chunks. This will help you see the specific steps you need to take to accomplish that goal.

From there, you can break each of the three chunks down further until they are ready to be turned into short-term marketing goals.

By focusing on your top priority and breaking it down into smaller, actionable steps, you'll be on your way to achieving your long-term marketing plan and making big progress in your small business.

CHAPTER 5:
Developing A Marketing Plan To Successfully Promote Your Product Or Service Online

"Every minute you spend in planning saves 10 minutes in execution. This gives you a 1,000 percent return on energy!"

— Brian Tracy

Why Is Developing A Marketing Plan Important?

Having a marketing plan is important because it helps you stay focused and on track when promoting your business.

Without a plan, you'll waste valuable time and resources on marketing tactics that don't work or aren't aligned with your business goals.

Here are five important reasons why you need a marketing plan:

1. **Clear and measurable goals and objectives**
   By setting clear and easy-to-measure goals, you can track progress and see how well your marketing is working.

2. **Use resources wisely**
   Find the best marketing channels and tactics so you can use your limited resources (time and money) efficiently.

3. **Keep an eye on trends and the competition**
   Stay informed about what's happening in your industry and what your competitors are doing, so you can not only keep up, but get ahead of them.

4. **Measure and evaluate results**
   Measure the success of your marketing efforts, like website visits, new leads, and sales. This helps you see what works and what doesn't, so you can change your plan if needed.

5. **Share your goals**
   A good plan helps you share your business goals with your team, partners, customers, and investors. By keeping them informed, they're more likely to help you reach your goals.

"What Happens If I Don't Develop A Marketing Plan?"

Without a plan, you may struggle to attract and retain customers, generate leads, and grow your business.

Here are a few potential downsides to consider:

- **Lack of focus**
  Without a plan, you may find yourself chasing after multiple marketing ideas at once, which can dilute your efforts and prevent you from achieving your business objectives.

- **Unclear goals**
  Without specific goals and metrics in place, it can be challenging to measure the success of your marketing efforts and make informed decisions about future investments.

- **Wasted resources**
  If you don't have a strong marketing plan, you may waste valuable time and money on marketing tactics that don't work or aren't aligned with your business goals.

- **Inconsistent messaging**
  Without a clear plan for your marketing efforts, you may send mixed messages to your target audience, which can lead to confusion and distrust.

- **Missed opportunities**
  Without a plan, you may not be able to take advantage of new marketing channels or tactics that could help you reach more customers.

===

In short, having a marketing plan is critical for small businesses that want to succeed in a competitive marketplace.

A solid plan helps you focus your efforts, optimize your resources, and achieve your business goals.

The Essential Elements Of Developing A Marketing Plan

A successful marketing plan for your small business needs to include the following:

1. **Executive summary**
   A high-level overview of your marketing plan and outline your business objectives, target audience, marketing channels, and budget.

2. **Market research**
   An in-depth understanding of your target market, including their demographics, behavior, and purchasing habits.

3. **Competitive analysis**
   Analyzes your competitors and identify their strengths, weaknesses, and marketing strategies.

4. **Your Unique Selling Proposition (USP)**
   Outlines your business's unique selling proposition, which is the value proposition that sets you apart from your competitors.

5. **Marketing strategy**
   Outlines your overall marketing strategy, including your target audience, messaging, and marketing channels.

6. **Marketing mix**
   Details the specific tactics and activities you will use to implement your marketing strategy, such as advertising, public relations, social media, and email marketing.

7. **Budget**
   Outlines your marketing budget and how you plan to allocate funds across various marketing channels and tactics.

8. **Metrics and analytics**
   Details the metrics and analytics you will use to measure the success of your marketing plan and make data-driven decisions.

9. **Implementation plan**
   Outlines the timeline and specific action steps for implementing your marketing plan.

10. **Contingency plan**
    Details how you'll adapt your marketing plan when (not if) external factors, such as changes in the market or competitive landscape, require you to pivot or adjust your strategy.

===

By including these essential elements in your marketing plan, you'll dramatically increase your chances of success and achieving your business objectives.

Developing A Marketing Plan Step-by-Step

The first version of your Marketing Plan doesn't have to be overcomplicated. In fact, you can fit it on a single piece of paper.

To create a marketing plan quickly and easily, focus on the following seven steps, and try to capture your answers in just 1 to 3 lines for each step.

Don't spend days or weeks researching each step in detail, but instead keep it simple and manageable so you can easily wrap your head around it.

Remember, your marketing plan is a living document that you will continue to improve and evolve over time.

STEP 1: Define your business objectives (30 minutes)

Spend time brainstorming and writing down three specific goals that you want to achieve through your marketing plan. Prioritize your goals in order of importance so you can focus your efforts on the most critical ones first.

STEP 2: Conduct market research (2 hours)

Researching your target audience to better understand their needs, preferences, and behaviors. Create a brief customer profile that includes basic demographic information, such as age, gender, and location, as well as lifestyle and behavioral characteristics, such as values, interests, and buying habits. (See "Chapter 2: Conducting Market Research")

STEP 3: Determine your unique selling proposition (15 minutes)

Define what makes your business special by identifying what you do differently than your competitors. This is called your "unique selling proposition", and it's what sets you apart and makes customers want to choose your business over others.

STEP 4: Choose marketing channels (1 hour)

Select the marketing channels that are most suitable for your target audience and align with your marketing goals. This could include digital channels like social media, email marketing, and online advertising, or more traditional channels like print ads, billboards, or TV commercials.

STEP 5: Set a marketing budget (1 hour)

Make the most of your marketing budget by dividing it thoughtfully across different marketing channels and tactics. This means identifying the most cost-effective channels and tactics to reach your target audience and investing more resources in those areas to maximize your return on investment.

STEP 6: Establish metrics and analytics (1 hour)

Decide on the key performance indicators (KPIs) that you will use to (a) measure how well your marketing plan is working, and (b) make smart decisions based on data. This could involve tracking website traffic, social media engagement, referrals, or sales figures.

STEP 7: Develop a content plan (2 hours)

Develop a plan for the content that you'll create and share across your marketing channels, such as social media posts, blog articles, and email newsletters.

Your content should align with your marketing objectives and be tailored to your target audience's needs and interests. This could involve brainstorming a few content ideas and creating an editorial calendar to help you stay on track.

===

By following these seven steps, you'll be able to create a comprehensive and effective marketing plan for your small business.

Remember to stay focused on your business objectives, differentiate yourself from your competitors, and measure the success of your marketing efforts. Good luck!

SPECIFIC SCENARIO: Caffeine Cove Café

Sam and Parker had been imaginary best friends since high school and always dreamed of starting a business together.

Their mutual love for coffee led them to open the equally imaginary "Caffeine Cove Café," a cozy coffee shop near the beach.

They were passionate about great coffee and focused on creating the perfect blends and a comfortable atmosphere for their customers.

However, during their first year in business, they struggled to attract a steady flow of customers and found it difficult to make ends meet.

Despite their dedication to quality coffee and great service, Sam and Parker realized that their initial success wasn't enough to sustain the business long-term.

They noticed that many potential customers simply didn't know about their café or what set it apart from other coffee shops.

It was then that they decided they needed a marketing plan to spread the word, attract more customers, and ultimately turn their struggling business around.

Here's the marketing plan Sam and Parker developed for the Caffeine Cove Café using the step-by-step checklist:

STEP 1: Define your business objectives (30 minutes)

Sam and Parker decided that their main objectives were increasing foot traffic, boosting sales of specific menu items, and expanding their customer base through targeted marketing efforts.

STEP 2: Conduct market research (2 hours)

After researching the demographics and psychographics of their target audience, they found that their ideal customers were primarily socially conscious millennials and Gen Z customers who valued sustainable, fair trade coffee and were willing to pay a premium for it.

STEP 3: Determine your unique selling proposition (15 minutes)

The duo identified Caffeine Cove Café's USP as their commitment to ethical sourcing, a cozy atmosphere, playing only music by local musicians and bands, using climate-friendly vendors, and offering the friendliest customer service in town.

STEP 4: Choose marketing channels (1 hour)

Sam and Parker decided to focus their marketing efforts on social media platforms like Instagram and Facebook, where they could showcase their shop's aesthetic and build an engaged community around the brand.

STEP 5: Set a marketing budget (1 hour)

They allocated 30% of their marketing budget to social media advertising, 20% to email marketing, and 50% to in-store promotions and events.

STEP 6: Establish metrics and analytics (1 hour)

To measure the success of Caffeine Cove Cafe's marketing efforts, Sam and Parker planned to track social media likes, website traffic, email coupon redemptions, and in-store sales.

They would then adjust each strategy accordingly based on what was working and what wasn't.

STEP 7: Develop a content plan (2 hours)

The co-owners crafted a content plan that included daily social media posts featuring their coffee and food offerings, weekly email newsletters highlighting new menu items and promotions, and in-store events such as coffee tasting workshops and performances by local musicians.

===

After implementing their marketing plan, Sam and Parker saw a significant improvement in Caffeine Cove Café's growth, customer engagement, and overall business results.

Foot traffic increased, sales of specific menu items soared, and their customer base expanded as a result of their targeted marketing efforts.

The carefully planned social media campaigns and in-store promotions attracted new customers, while the engaging email newsletters helped retain existing ones.

By focusing on their unique selling proposition and adjusting their strategies based on analytics, Sam and Parker successfully turned their coffee shop into a thriving business that became a popular spot in their community.

Strategy Snapshot For Developing A Marketing Plan

Developing a marketing plan is crucial for the success of your small business.

Start by defining your marketing goals and identifying specific objectives you want to achieve through your marketing plan. This will help you to stay focused and aligned with your business objectives.

After setting your goals, conduct research on your target audience, which will help you understand their needs, preferences, and behaviors.

It's important to identify your unique selling proposition, which is what sets your business apart from competitors.

Once you've defined your USP, choose the marketing channels that best align with your marketing objectives and target audience.

To measure your marketing plan's success, decide on the key performance metrics that you'll use to track your progress and make data-driven decisions.

Finally, create a content plan that aligns with your marketing objectives and target audience's needs and interests.

By including these sections, you will develop a marketing plan that gets you closer to your business goals. Refer back to your plan over and over again and improve upon it each time.

Take The First Step

Grab a piece of paper or open a new document and brainstorm a few marketing objectives that you want to achieve in the short-term and long-term.

For example, you might want to increase website traffic, boost social media engagement, or generate more leads.

Once you have a list of objectives, prioritize them based on importance and select one or two goals that you want to achieve in the next few weeks or months. Write down these goals and a few ideas for how you can achieve them.

This could involve developing content for social media, launching an email marketing campaign, or trying out a new advertising channel.

By setting specific goals and identifying actionable steps to achieve them, you'll start the process of building your marketing plan immediately.

Chapter 6:

How To Create Powerful Marketing Messages That Command Attention And Boost Sales

"I've learned that people will forget what you said, people will forget what you did, but people will never forget how you made them feel."

— Maya Angelou

Why Is It Important To Learn To Create Powerful Marketing Messages?

Creating powerful marketing messages is a key skill for small business owners who want to grow their customer base, increase sales, and differentiate themselves from the competition.

By mastering this skill, you can construct compelling and persuasive messaging that resonates with your target audience and helps you achieve your business goals.

Learning how to create powerful marketing messages enables you and your team to:

1. **Reach your target audience**
   When you compose messages in a way that speaks directly to your ideal customers, you create a connection with the people who are most likely to buy from you.

2. **Establish credibility**
   Messaging that shows your expertise and experience can establish trust with potential customers and make them more likely to choose you over other businesses.

3. **Gain a competitive edge**
   By mastering the skill of creating persuasive messages, you can set yourself apart from the competition and become a go-to choice for potential customers.

4. **Increase website traffic**
   Marketing messages that are interesting and engaging can drive more people to your website, which can mean more sales for you.

5. **Generate leads**
   When you write or speak in a compelling way, you attract new leads and prospects to your business, giving you more opportunities to grow your customer base.

6. **Boost sales**
   Good messaging can persuade people to buy your products and services. That means you're making their lives better while generating more cash flow for your small business.

7. **Build long-term customer relationships**
   When your messaging helps solve your target market's problems, you build trust and credibility with them. That creates stronger relationships with them and gives them an incentive to keep coming back for more content, and ultimately, more products and services.

"What Happens If I Don't Learn To Create Powerful Marketing Messages?"

Without mastering the art of creating powerful marketing messages, you may face negative consequences that can stunt your revenue and growth, including:

- **Limited Reach**
  If your messages aren't effective, they won't reach the people who are most likely to buy from you, which means you'll miss out on serving potential customers.

- **Inconsistent Branding**
  Bad messaging creates confusion and ends up hurting your brand.

  For example, imagine a smoothie shop with a website that says, "Enjoy the best smoothies in town! Our fruits are sourced from local farms and blended to purr-fection. Stop by our pet-friendly shop and try our new mango-catnip smoothie!"

  The mixed messages in this poorly written copy might confuse potential customers, making them unsure if the shop specializes in high-quality smoothies or if it's a quirky, cat-themed café.

  This confusion could deter people from visiting the smoothie shop, ultimately hurting the brand's reputation and growth.

- **Lack of Differentiation**
  Without messaging that showcases what makes you different, your business blends in with the competition and fails to convert prospects who are on the fence.

- **Negative Reputation**
  Poor messaging makes your business look unprofessional and untrustworthy, which can often damage your reputation.

- **Decreased Sales**
  If you can't convey your thoughts and ideas in an engaging, persuasive manner, your business will struggle to attract and retain customers, leading to lost revenue.

===

Developing the skill of creating powerful marketing messages offers a range of advantages to your small business.

You'll be able to avoid the pitfalls of poor communication and differentiate yourself in a competitive market, leading to increased customer acquisition, retention rates, and growth.

The Essential Elements Of Creating Powerful Marketing Messages

In a competitive marketplace, you need to create effective marketing messages that communicate the unique value of your products and services.

Here are 10 essential elements to crafting powerful marketing messages:

1. **Address your target market**
   Speak directly to your target market, as if you're best friends, and address their needs and desires.

2. **Highlight your Unique Selling Proposition (USP)**
   Showcase what sets your products and services apart from the competition and why they're different.

3. **Explain the benefits**
   Clearly and concisely explain the benefits of your products and services and how they can improve the lives of your customers. By talking about the problems you're solving for them, you're proving that you understand them. Everyone wants to feel heard.

4. **Create emotional appeal**
   Connect with your target market emotionally and evoke positive feelings that drive them to take action.

5. **Keep it short and to the point**
   Use concise language that's easy to understand and keep your messages short and to the point. People are busy and want to get to the point quickly. Even when you're creating long-form messages (videos, podcasts, pillar articles, etc.), don't belabor each point or repeat yourself unnecessarily.

6. **Ensure clarity**
   Avoid jargon or confusing language that might turn off potential customers. Make sure your messages are easy to understand.

7. **Maintain your brand voice**
   Align your messages with your brand voice and personality to create a consistent experience for your target market, or else you'll risk confusing and alienating your audience.

8. **Be authentic**
   Ensure that your messages are truthful and authentic, avoiding misleading or false claims that can damage your reputation (or worse, cause you to get sued).

9. **Include a clear call to action**
   Make sure your messages include a clear and compelling call to action that tells your audience EXACTLY what to do next.

10. **Test and optimize**
    Continually test and optimize your messages with your target market to see what resonates with them and what doesn't. Adjust and optimize

your messaging to ensure that it's effective, making changes as needed to improve performance.

Writing Powerful Marketing Messages Step-by-Step

Here's an example of a poorly written marketing message: "We offer the best service in town. Contact us today."

Let's transform this into a *powerful* marketing message, step by step, based on the Essential Elements listed in the previous section of this chapter.

STEP 1: Use an attention-grabbing headline

Capture your target market's attention with a headline that is concise and compelling. Use language that speaks to their pain points and offers a solution.

For example, "How To Get [good thing] Without [bad thing]". (e.g., "How To Get Luxury Services Without Going Broke Paying For Them")

STEP 2: Define your unique selling proposition (USP)

What sets your service apart from the competition? Is it your experience, expertise, or customer service? Identify your unique selling proposition and make sure it's highlighted in your marketing message.

For example, "We pride ourselves on being the only company in town that offers a 100% satisfaction guarantee on this particular service. If you're not completely satisfied with our service, we'll make it right or give you your money back."

STEP 3: Call out your target market

Who are you trying to reach with your marketing message? Call out to them directly so they know your message is customized for them.

For example, "If you're a busy professional who needs reliable and hassle-free service for your home office, this is exactly what you've been waiting for."

STEP 4: Provide benefits, not just features

Don't just list the features of your service, explain how those features benefit your customers.

For example, instead of saying "Our service includes 24/7 customer support" (which is only a feature), say "Our 24/7 customer support ensures that you'll never be left in the dark when you need help the most" (which states the feature followed by the benefit).

STEP 5: Use persuasive language

Use persuasive language throughout your marketing message, such as phrases that evoke emotions.

Some examples: "Are you tired of unreliable service providers?", "Experience the peace of mind that comes with our dependable service", and "Join the thousands of satisfied customers who trust us with their service needs."

STEP 6: Include social proof

Include testimonials, case studies, or other forms of social proof in your marketing message. This can help build trust with potential customers and increase the likelihood that they'll convert.

For example, "See below for what our satisfied customers have to say about our exceptional service."

STEP 7: Address objections

Don't wait until after your messaging to address objections. Include the common objections or concerns that potential customers may have (based on your past customer service experiences). By addressing the common concerns in your copy, you will alleviate their fears and increase the likelihood they'll buy from you.

For example, "Worried about the cost? Our team will work with you to create a personalized plan that fits your unique situation, so you can get the most value out of our services without breaking the bank."

STEP 8: Include a call-to-action (CTA)

Include a clear call-to-action in your marketing message that tells potential customers what action to take next.

For example, "Contact us today to schedule your hassle-free service appointment."

STEP 9: Test and optimize

Test different variations of your marketing message to see what resonates best with your target audience.

Use A/B testing* to experiment with different headlines, language, and CTAs. Optimize your message based on the results to increase conversions (from strangers to prospects, or prospects to customers) and return on investment (ROI) for your marketing costs.

===

*NOTE: A/B testing, also known as split-testing, is where you send one message to a portion of your audience, and a similar-but-slightly-different message to a different portion of your audience. The purpose is to see which message resonates the most.

If half your audience sees "Message A" and buys your product or service, and the other half sees "Message B" and doesn't buy, it's clear that "Message A" is the best message to increase sales.

It's best to test one thing at a time, like the color of a postcard, or the subject line of an email message. Based on the responses you get, pick a winner and then split-test the winner against a new, third message (for example, "Message A" versus "Message C"). Rinse and repeat.

Follow these steps to transform any poorly constructed marketing message into one that is powerful, persuasive, and effective.

SPECIFIC SCENARIO: The Study Squad

A pretend company called "The Study Squad" wants to reach out to parents of high-school kids to tell them about their tutoring services.

In the past, their marketing message consisted of a simple postcard with the words "Get better grades with The Study Squad. We're the best tutoring service around. Contact us today!"

As you can see, their message doesn't address their target market or their needs, and it doesn't provide any benefits or reasons why they are the "best tutoring service around".

After seeing our approach to writing powerful marketing messages, they decided to send out flyers instead of postcards because they needed additional room to share their message.

Here's how it turned out, using the step-by-step checklist in the previous section:

STEP 1: Use an attention-grabbing headline

"How To Boost Your High Schooler's Grades Without Sacrificing Family Time"

STEP 2: Define your unique selling proposition (USP)

"At The Study Squad, we know that every student is unique, and that's why our approach is personalized to fit your individual learning needs. Our expert tutors work with you to create a customized study plan that targets your child's specific areas of need, giving them the tools they need to succeed."

STEP 3: Call out your target audience

"If you're a parent of a high-school student who is struggling with learning and earning good grades, we understand the challenges you face. The Study Squad is here to help, with tutoring services designed boost your child's confidence and academic performance."

STEP 4: Provide benefits, not just features

"Our expert tutors don't just teach subjects — they teach students. We focus on building foundational knowledge and study skills that your child can carry with them throughout their academic career and beyond. With The Study Squad, your child will not only improve their grades but also develop the tools they need to become lifelong learners."

STEP 5: Use persuasive language

"Get ready to see results! The Study Squad will give your child personalized attention, targeted instruction, and the resources they need to improve their grades. Our expert tutors use engaging, interactive teaching methods that make learning fun and effective."

STEP 6: Address objections

"We know you may have concerns about tutoring services, but with The Study Squad, there's no need to worry. Our expert tutors are vetted and experienced, and we offer a satisfaction guarantee to give you peace of mind. Plus, with flexible scheduling and online tutoring options, we make it easy to fit tutoring into your busy schedule."

STEP 7: Provide social proof

"Don't just take our word for it — check out our testimonials from satisfied parents and students. Our proven track record of success speaks for itself, with student report cards showing a jump of one to two grade points on average, which in turn creates self-confidence in their academic abilities."

STEP 8: Include a clear call to action

"Ready to see the difference The Study Squad can make for your child? Call us today at 1-800-555-5555 to schedule a consultation and learn more about how we can help your child succeed."

===

After implementing the step-by-step checklist for writing a powerful marketing message, the fictional Study Squad has seen fictionally incredible results.

Parents of high-school students in their area are now more aware of the benefits that come with their personalized tutoring services. They realize that The Study Squad's experienced team is dedicated to helping their children reach their full potential.

Strategy Snapshot For Writing Powerful Marketing Messages

In today's competitive market, it's essential to create powerful marketing messages that grab your audience's attention and persuade them to take action.

Effectively crafted marketing messages can help your business stand out from the competition, engage with your target audience, and ultimately convert leads and prospects into customers.

To create a powerful marketing message, it's important to first identify the target audience and speak directly to them.

Use attention-grabbing headlines and persuasive language to capture their attention and make them want to learn more about the product or service being offered.

It's also important to clearly communicate the benefits of the product or service and address any objections the target audience may have.

Social proof, such as customer testimonials or case studies, can help build trust and credibility with potential customers.

A clear call to action should be included in every marketing message, encouraging the target audience to take the next step in the customer journey.

Finally, regular testing and optimization can help improve the effectiveness of the marketing message over time.

By following these steps, your small business can create powerful marketing messages that resonate with your target market and drive conversions.

Take The First Step

The most important thing you can do right now before you start writing powerful marketing messages is to focus on your unique selling proposition (USP), aka "Essential Element #2".

Identify what sets your product or service apart from the competition, write it down in a clear and concise way, and make sure it's visible in all your marketing materials.

This will help you stand out from the crowd and attract the attention of your target market.

Take some time right now to capture your USP in writing and start incorporating it into all your marketing messages.

Chapter 7:
Why Using Social Media For Marketing Is The Ultimate Game Changer

"It's a dialogue, not a monologue, and some people don't understand that. Social media is more like a telephone than a television."

— Amy Jo Martin

Why Is Using Social Media For Marketing Important?

Social media is a great way to get your message out there and connect with people who are interested in what you have to offer.

By sharing your content on platforms like Facebook, YouTube, LinkedIn, Instagram, Pinterest, and more, you can reach a wider audience and build a following of people who are excited about your brand.

One of the best things about social media is that it's a two-way street. You can share your content with your followers, but you can also engage with them by having digital conversations and liking and sharing their posts.

By doing so, you can build relationships with your audience and show them that you care about what they have to say.

Here are a few of the benefits that social media offers when it comes to marketing:

1. **Get more attention**
   Online platforms help you get noticed by more people, which increases the awareness of your brand. With the right message, a social media post may even go viral, helping you reach hundreds, thousands, or even millions more people than you normally would.

2. **Showcase your expertise**
   Social media provides a platform for you to share your knowledge and expertise with your followers. By sharing helpful tips and advice related to your industry, you can position yourself (and your brand) as a thought leader, which helps you build trust and credibility with your audience.

3. **Talk directly to your target market**
   Online platforms make it easier for you to chat directly with customers and prospects, whether they are located nearby or from around the world. Most online platforms have tools to help you find and talk to the people who are most likely to buy from you.

4. **Reduce your marketing expenses**
   Social media marketing is often much less expensive than traditional marketing and advertising. You can reallocate those savings into other parts of your business.

5. **Show up higher in search results**
   Being active online helps you establish a digital footprint. Creating footprints on multiple social media platforms can help you appear higher in search engine results, making it easier for people to find you — and your offerings.

6. **Compete with bigger businesses**
   Online marketing can help your small business compete with bigger businesses by giving you a way to reach a lot of people at no cost (or on a small budget). There are individual influencers online that have a larger following than many public companies.

For example, as of this writing, popular influencer Jimmy Donaldson, aka "MrBeast", has 8X more YouTube subscribers (and 24X more video views) than Apple, the $2.5 Trillion, publicly traded, computer and multimedia corporation. (source: www.YouTube.com)

7. **Learn more about your target market**
Online platforms can provide you with specific information about what your customers like and want, which helps you improve your products and services.

8. **Build loyal followers and customers**
Social media can help you build strong, long-lasting relationships with your existing customers, which often encourages them to come back and buy more.

9. **Stay top of mind**
By regularly posting on social media, you can keep your brand top-of-mind for your followers. This means that when they need a product or service that you offer, they are more likely to think of you and your company.

10. **Encourage user-generated content**
You can engage with your audience and encourage them to create and share content related to your brand. This can result in user-generated content that you can then share on your own platforms, which can help increase your reach and credibility.

"What Happens If I Don't Use Social Media For Marketing?"

For the vast majority of small businesses, social media has become a required tool for connecting with their customers and staying competitive.

Without it, you will likely miss multiple opportunities to grow. Here are a few of the dangers of not using social media for marketing:

- **Reduced brand awareness**
  By not using social media, you're limiting your ability to reach a wider audience and build brand awareness.

- **Falling behind the competition**
  If your competitors are using social media to market their products and services, you risk falling behind and losing market share.

- **Limited customer engagement**
  Social media provides a platform for businesses to engage with customers and build relationships, so not using it can limit your ability to connect with your audience.

- **Lower customer retention**
  Without social media, you may struggle to keep your customers engaged and interested in your products and services, leading to lower retention rates.

- **Inability to monitor online reputation**
  Social media provides a way for businesses to monitor what is being said about their brand online and respond to negative comments or reviews. Not using social media can mean missing out on these opportunities to manage your online reputation.

- **Limited customer feedback**
  Social media provides a way for businesses to receive feedback from their customers, which can be valuable for improving products and services. Not using social media can limit your ability to receive feedback from your customers.

- **Less effective marketing**
  Without social media, you may have to rely on less effective marketing strategies, such as print ads or direct mail, which can be more expensive and have a lower return on investment (ROI).

- **Missed opportunities for collaboration**
  Social media provides a way for businesses to collaborate with other businesses and influencers, which can be valuable for building partnerships and reaching new audiences. Not using social media can mean missing out on these opportunities for collaboration.

- **Difficulty reaching younger audiences**
  Younger generations are more likely to use social media as their primary

source of information and communication, so not using social media can make it difficult for you to reach this demographic.

===

Using social media for marketing allows you to reach a larger audience, build brand awareness, and connect with your target market in a cost-effective way.

It also enables you to gather valuable data on customer behavior and preferences to refine your marketing strategy and ultimately drive sales.

The Essential Elements Of Using Social Media For Marketing

With so many social media platforms out there, it can be overwhelming for small businesses to know where to start with their social media marketing.

While each platform is unique in its own way, there are some essential elements for using social media for marketing that work across multiple platforms and are essentially timeless.

You can use these to build an effective social media marketing strategy that can be adapted to various platforms and changes in the social media landscape.

1. **Understand your target market**
   Knowing your target audience and what they want is key to creating content that resonates with them and engages them regardless of the platform you're using.

2. **Consistent brand voice and visual style**
   Consistency in your brand's voice and visual style across all social media platforms can help increase brand recognition and establish trust with your audience.

3. **Engaging content**
   Posting content that is interesting, informative, and occasionally provocative will help keep your audience interested in your brand and encourage them to connect with you.

4. **Active engagement with your audience**
   Responding to comments and messages in a timely manner and engaging with your audience through digital conversations, likes, and shares can help build strong relationships with your followers.

5. **Effective use of hashtags**
   #Hashtags are a universal feature for most (if not all) social media platforms. Using relevant and strategic hashtags can help your content reach a wider audience and increase engagement. (Most platforms recommend 3-5 hashtags, although some allow more.)

6. **Visual content**
   Wherever possible, including visual content like images and videos in your social media posts can help increase engagement and make your content more shareable. After all, a picture's worth 1,000 words.

7. **Consistent posting schedule**
   Posting content regularly can help keep your audience engaged and interested in your brand.

8. **Monitoring analytics**
   Regularly using social media analytics to track your results is a great way to see what's working and what isn't. Fine-tuning and adjusting your strategy can help you optimize your social media marketing efforts for even better results.

9. **Cross-promotion**
   Share your social media on your website and in ads. Share your website on your social media. This helps get more visitors and followers everywhere.

10. **Staying up-to-date with social media trends**
    Keeping up with the latest social media trends and updates can help you stay ahead of the curve and adapt your strategy to the inevitable changes in the social media landscape.

Using Social Media For Marketing Step-by-Step

Social media has become an integral part of marketing for businesses of all sizes. With so many platforms and strategies to choose from, it can be overwhelming to know where to start.

To help you get started, here are 10 actionable steps you can take to start effectively using social media for marketing.

These steps are designed to help you engage with your audience, create valuable content, and build brand awareness on various social media platforms.

By incorporating these tactics into your social media strategy, you can help grow your business and increase your reach online.

STEP 1: Choose which social media platform(s) to prioritize based on where your target market spends most of their time (1 hour)

Do some research to determine which social media platforms your target audience is most active on, and prioritize those platforms in your social media strategy. This will help you reach the right people and maximize the impact of your social media marketing efforts. It will also reduce wasting time on platforms your target market barely uses.

STEP 2: Create engaging content (1-2 hours)

Write a 200-word blog post or record a 3-minute video on your phone that addresses one of your target market's biggest pain points and provides a solution.

Post it on one of your social media platforms, and include a call to action (CTA) at the end that encourages readers/viewers to leave a comment and share the post with their friends.

STEP 3: Engage with your audience (30 minutes)

Respond to comments and messages in a timely manner, and engage with your audience through likes and shares. This helps build strong relationships and create a sense of community around your brand.

STEP 4: Establish a consistent posting schedule (1 hour)

Spend an hour creating a content calendar for the next month. Plan out at least two posts per week, and schedule them in advance to ensure consistency.

STEP 5: Know your numbers (15 minutes a week)

Schedule a 15-minute block of time each week to review your social media analytics to find potential areas for improvement.

Look for patterns in engagement, follower growth, reach, and what types of content are most popular. Use this information to refine your social media strategy.

STEP 6: Collaborate with influencers (2-3 hours)

Research influencers in your industry or niche and reach out to them to see if they would be interested in collaborating with your brand on social media. Many will say "no", and that's okay. You only need one good "yes" to dramatically increase your number of followers.

STEP 7: Run a social media contest (2-3 hours)

Create a social media contest that encourages user-generated content and offers a prize for the winner. Promote the contest on your social media channels to increase participation.

STEP 8: Offer social media-exclusive promotions (1 hour)

Offer an exclusive, followers-only discount or promotion to your social media followers to encourage engagement and loyalty.

STEP 9: Share customer success stories (30 minutes)

Share stories of your satisfied customers on social media to build trust and establish social proof for your brand.

STEP 10: Join one social media group (1 hour a week)

Find a relevant social media group (on LinkedIn or Facebook or other platform) where you can engage with other members by answering questions and sharing thought leadership content.

SPECIFIC SCENARIO: Breathtaking Baby Buggies

Meet Maria Castillo, a young and fictional mother of two toddlers who is also the founder of a fictional small business called Breathtaking Baby Buggies.

As a mom and an influencer in the baby carriage niche, she knows firsthand how important it is to provide the ultimate comfort and safety for little ones. That's why she invented a luxurious and innovative baby buggy that is truly a work of art.

However, she also knows that having a great product is not enough; she needs to effectively market her product to her target audience.

Luckily, social media offers her the perfect platform to reach out to her customers and increase sales.

In this hypothetical, step-by-step example, we will share how Maria is using social media for marketing her Breathtaking Baby Buggies.

STEP 1: Choose which social media platform(s) to prioritize based on where your target market spends most of their time (1 hour)

Maria decides to prioritize Facebook since it's where over 81% of millennial moms spend their time.

STEP 2: Create engaging content (1-2 hours)

She writes a blog post titled "10 Features That Make Breathtaking Baby Buggies Stand Out" that addresses common pain points and concerns of new parents when it comes to purchasing baby carriages.

The post highlights the unique features and benefits of her product and includes a call to action at the end, inviting readers to visit her website to learn more.

STEP 3: Engage with your audience (30 minutes)

Maria responds promptly to comments on her Facebook page and encourages her followers to share their own experiences with Breathtaking Baby Buggies.

She also shares photos and videos of happy customers using her product and includes a CTA asking her followers to share their own photos and experiences.

STEP 4: Establish a consistent posting schedule (1 hour)

She spends an hour creating a content calendar for the next month, planning out two posts per week. She decides to post every Monday and Thursday and schedules posts in advance to ensure consistency.

STEP 5: Know Your Numbers (15 minutes a week)

Every week, Maria checks her Facebook Insights to see which posts are getting the most engagement from her audience.

By regularly reviewing her social media analytics, she gains insights into what type of content resonates with her audience and adjusts her social media strategy accordingly.

After analyzing the data for the past week, she discovers that posts about shock-absorbing wheels (to ensure a smooth ride over even the bumpiest terrains) are receiving three times as many likes, comments, and shares than any other type of post.

She decides to create more content around the benefits of shock-absorbing wheels, and commits to incorporate more of this messaging into her other posts as well.

STEP 6: Collaborate with influencers (2-3 hours)

Maria researches influencers in the baby carriage niche and reaches out to them to see if they would be interested in collaborating with Breathtaking Baby Buggies on social media. She also considers offering a discount code to their followers to encourage them to try her product.

STEP 7: Run a social media contest (2-3 hours)

She creates a social media contest that encourages user-generated content and offers a free Breathtaking Baby Buggy as the prize.

Maria then promotes the contest on her Facebook page and encourages her followers to participate by sharing photos of their own Breathtaking Baby Buggy and tagging her page.

STEP 8: Offer social media-exclusive promotions (1 hour)

To show her appreciation for her Facebook followers, Maria offers a limited-time, 10% discount off all Breathtaking Baby Buggies.

She's thrilled to share this exclusive promotion with her loyal followers and hopes to attract new customers as well. She spreads the word on Facebook and encourages her followers to take advantage of the discount while it lasts.

STEP 9: Share customer success stories (30 minutes)

Maria shares stories of her satisfied customers on her Facebook page to build trust and establish social proof for her brand.

She highlights how her product has made a positive impact on their lives as parents and encourages others to share their own stories.

STEP 10: Join one social media group (1 hour a week)

Maria joins a Facebook group for new parents and engages with other members by answering questions and sharing her own experiences and thought leadership content related to baby carriages.

She establishes herself as a trusted expert in the industry and builds relationships with potential customers.

===

By following this step-by-step process, Maria Castillo was able to effectively use social media for marketing her Breathtaking Baby Buggies to her target audience.

Strategy Snapshot For Using Social Media For Marketing

Using social media for marketing gives you a powerful tool to reach your target market and increase sales.

To effectively market your services and products on social media, start by choosing the platforms where your target market hangs out.

Create engaging content that addresses their pain points and provides solutions.

Be sure to engage with your audience by responding to comments and messages in a timely manner, and establish a consistent posting schedule to maintain brand visibility.

Review your social media analytics regularly to gain insights and refine your social media strategy accordingly.

Collaborate with influencers, run social media contests, and offer social media-exclusive promotions to build engagement and loyalty.

Share customer success stories to establish social proof and trust with your audience.

Finally, join relevant social media groups to network with other professionals in your industry and establish yourself as a thought leader.

Take The First Step

The most important thing you can do right now to make progress in your social media marketing is to establish a consistent posting schedule.

Spend an hour creating a content calendar for the next month, planning at least two posts per week, and schedule them in advance to ensure consistency.

This will help you build brand recognition, increase engagement, and attract potential customers.

So take out your calendar, block off an hour, and get started on creating a consistent posting schedule for your social media accounts today.

Chapter 8:
How To Create Successful Email Marketing Campaigns That Convert

"If you love someone, set them free. If they don't come back, put them in a 21-day drip campaign."

— Rohit Srivastav

Why Is It Important To Create Successful Email Marketing Campaigns?

Imagine you've been sharing awesome stuff on social media for a really long time.

Your posts are enjoyable, informative, and sometimes even life-changing for your followers. You've worked hard for over three years to build a loyal following of more than 225,000 people on one platform alone.

But one day, when you try to log in to that platform, you find that you've been locked out!

The platform's new terms might have caused this, or maybe you just forgot your password. Either way, it's a bummer because now you can't connect with the 225,000 followers you worked so hard to gather.

It's possible that you'll regain access in a day, a week, or after a few months, but it's also possible you might NEVER regain access to that account.

If not, that's three years of hard work down the drain. You'll have to start all over again from scratch.

And while this story isn't real, it's something that happens to small business owners every day. In fact, a recent Google search of "locked out of social media" resulted in a whopping 271 million results!

This is why it's so risky to rely solely on traffic that you don't own.

While it's true that social media can be an excellent way to reach a large audience, the risk of losing that audience due to unforeseen circumstances such as account hacking or platform changes can be a major setback.

For those reasons and more, building an email list is a very valuable asset for any small business owner. You don't have to worry about being at the mercy of your social media platform.

Mastering the art and science of email marketing to that list will help you grow your business predictably and reliably.

Here are some of the many advantages of creating successful email marketing campaigns that are unique to email and more powerful than social media marketing:

1. **High ROI**
   Email marketing has one of the highest returns on investment (ROI) of any marketing channel. According to Forbes, email marketing can generate an average ROI of $42 for every $1 spent. (source: http://www.forbes.com/sites/allbusiness/2020/10/26/email-marketing-still-the-most-powerful-tool-to-take-your-business-to-the-next-level)

   Compare that to social media: As of this writing, the average ROI for social media is about $2.80 for every $1 spent. That means email is outperforming social media by a ratio of 15:1 ($42 divided by $2.80). (source: https://nealschaffer.com/social-media-roi)

2. **Direct communication**
   Email marketing allows you to communicate directly with your audience, without any interference from algorithms or platform changes.

3. **Targeted messaging**
   With email marketing, you can segment your list and send targeted messages to specific groups of subscribers based on their interests, behavior, or demographic information.

4. **Personalization**
   Email marketing allows you to personalize your messages with the recipient's name, location, or other relevant information, which can significantly increase engagement and conversions.

5. **Automation**
   Email marketing automation allows you to set up automated campaigns that trigger based on specific actions or behaviors, such as abandoned cart reminders, welcome series, or birthday offers.

6. **Longer lifespan**
   Unlike social media posts that disappear quickly, emails have a longer lifespan and can remain in a recipient's inbox for days, weeks, or even months.

7. **Higher conversion rates**
   Email marketing has been shown to be more effective than social media marketing when it comes to conversion rates, as subscribers who receive emails are more likely to take action and make a purchase.

"What Happens If I Don't Create Successful Email Marketing Campaigns?"

If you focus solely on social media and neglect building successful email marketing campaigns, your business will suffer for it.

Here are a few of the negative consequences that happen without email marketing:

- **Less data**
  Without email marketing, you miss out on the opportunity to gather and control valuable customer data, such as email addresses, phone numbers (for SMS marketing), purchasing habits, and preferences.

- **Non-personalized messaging**
  Not using email marketing means missed opportunities to provide personalized experiences for your audience. For example, you can't address people by name, and you can't personalize by gender, age, or hobbies, assuming they've voluntarily given you that info. (Note: Paid advertising on social media allows for some personalization, but you have to pay to personalize. And even then, it's not nearly as personalized as you can get with free email segmentation.)

- **Limited lead nurturing**
  Without an email marketing campaign, you'll miss out on opportunities to automate the nurturing of new leads to guide them towards a purchase.

- **Misaligned messaging**
  Without email, it's hard to segment your list and send tailored messages to each group based on their interests (for example, dog lovers versus cat lovers). Social media messages go out to all your followers, and often doesn't resonate with large segments of them, making them feel unheard and unseen.

- **Limited loyalty**
  The more channels you can use to connect with prospects and customers, the stronger the bond you'll have with them. Without leveraging email, it will be harder to build loyalty and retain customers.

- **Lower ROI**
  Email marketing has a high return on investment (ROI) for small businesses. Not using email marketing means missing out on this potential ROI.

- **Limited opportunities for testing and optimization**
  Email marketing allows you to test and optimize different messages and content strategies based on segmentation. Not using email limits those opportunities.

Successful email marketing campaigns provide a powerful way to connect with your audience and build relationships with your customers. They help accelerate the growth of your business.

The Essential Elements Of Creating Successful Email Marketing Campaigns

Email marketing has become an increasingly important tool for businesses of all sizes to connect with their audience, build relationships, and drive revenue.

Successful email marketing campaigns can provide a high return on investment and help you achieve your growth goals, whether it's through generating leads, promoting products and services, or nurturing customer loyalty.

However, with so many emails flooding inboxes, it's essential to have a strategy that stands out and delivers value to your list.

Let's explore 10 essential elements of successful email marketing campaigns that can help you optimize your strategy and achieve your business objectives.

1. **Suspenseful subject lines**
   Your email subject lines should be concise, compelling, and create curiosity, grabbing the recipient's attention and encouraging them to open the email.

2. **Engaging content**
   The content of your emails should be engaging, informative, and relevant to the recipient's interests, providing value and building trust.

3. **Strong call-to-action**
   Every email should have a clear call-to-action (CTA), prompting the recipient to take a specific action, such as watching a video, downloading a free resource, signing up for a free trial, or making a purchase.

4. **Mobile responsiveness**
   Check to make sure your emails are mobile-responsive, ensuring they looks good and function well on different devices and screen sizes.

5. **Personalization**
   Personalizing your emails with the recipient's name, location, and other relevant information increases engagement and conversions.

6. **Segmentation**
   Segment your email list and send targeted messages to specific groups based on their interests, behavior, and/or demographics to increase relevance and engagement.

7. **Timing**
   Timing your messages for optimal delivery increases open and click-through rates. Experiment with sending on different days and at different times to find what works best for your audience.

8. **Visuals**
   Adding visual elements such as images, animated GIFs, or short infographics enhances the appeal of your emails and makes them more engaging.

9. **Social sharing**
   Including social sharing buttons in your email encourages recipients to share your content with their followers, expanding your reach and potential audience.

10. **Metrics and analysis**
    Regularly tracking and analyzing your email metrics, such as open rates, click-through rates, and conversion rates, can help you optimize your campaigns for better results.

    Note: Some of these metrics are getting harder to track depending on the recipient's email client, but adding UTM tags* to your links sometimes helps.

    *Learn more about UTM tags at
    https://en.wikipedia.org/wiki/UTM_parameters

Create Successful Email Marketing Campaigns Step-by-Step

Creating a successful email marketing campaign is an effective way to connect with your audience, build relationships, and drive revenue.

Whether you're new to email marketing or looking to refine your approach, this step-by-step checklist will guide you through building your next email marketing campaign.

STEP 1: Define your marketing campaign objectives (15 minutes)

Set specific goals for your email campaign series, such as generating leads, promoting a specific product or service, or nurturing customer loyalty. This will help you focus your efforts and measure success.

STEP 2: Segment your email list for the campaign (2-4 hours if not already segmented)

Divide your email list into smaller groups based on common demographics, interests, and/or behaviors for each group. This allows you to send targeted messages that are more relevant to each segment.

STEP 3: Outline your email campaign journey (1 hour)

Create a plan for your email campaign series, including how many messages (3-10 is ideal), how long a time period (3 days? 3 weeks? somewhere in between?), average message length (short, medium, or long), sending cadence (every day? twice a week?), and what elements you'll need (videos? case studies? testimonials?).

Plan your messaging so that it takes your recipients on a journey over the course of the campaign, including a beginning, middle, and end. Develop a list of topics for each email that will help guide your content creation process.

STEP 4: Write your email campaign content (15 minutes per email)

Craft engaging, personalized content for each email in your series. Use visuals such as images or videos to make your message more engaging.

STEP 5: Create intriguing subject lines for each email (5 minutes per email)

Craft a captivating subject line for each email that accurately reflects its content, yet piques the recipient's curiosity and motivates them to open it. A great subject line should be interesting, intriguing, and leave the recipient wanting to know more.

STEP 6: Add strong calls-to-action for each email (5 minutes per email)

Include a clear and compelling call-to-action in each email that prompts the recipient to take a specific action, such as making a purchase, signing up for a free trial, or visiting your website.

STEP 7: Optimize your emails for mobile (5 minutes per email)

Make sure each email is mobile-responsive and looks good on different devices and screen sizes. This will ensure that your message is accessible to a wider audience.

STEP 8: Choose a send day and time for each email (1 minute per email)

Experiment with different sending times to find the optimal time for each email in your series. Consider factors such as time zone, day of the week, and the recipient's work schedule.

STEP 9: Automate the campaign (1-2 hours)

Don't send out your emails manually via your personal email client. A good email service provider (ESP) will let you automate your entire campaign.

Just upload your email list, use tags for segmenting your list, copy and paste each message, set a sending schedule, and start the campaign to your existing list.

For new leads, you can set the ESP to automatically put them into the campaign starting on Day 1, making the entire process completely hands-off once the email marketing campaign has been set up correctly.

STEP 10: Analyze the data and refine each message (1 hour per week)

Track your email metrics, such as open rates, click-through rates, and conversion rates for each email in your series, and use the data to refine your approach. Identify areas for improvement and test new strategies to optimize your campaign.

===

With these steps, you can create well-planned-out and successful email marketing campaigns that are engaging, personalized, and effective in achieving your business objectives.

Keep in mind there is no single "right" way to create an email marketing campaign. Instead, focus on testing different approaches, collecting data, and making incremental improvements with each campaign you send out.

By analyzing your results and making small adjustments over time, you can optimize your campaign and achieve better results.

The key is to keep experimenting and learning, using each campaign as an opportunity to refine your approach and get closer to your marketing goals.

SPECIFIC SCENARIO: Workoutopia

Kwame Johnson is an imaginary fitness coach who has always had a passion for helping people achieve their health and wellness goals.

He combines cardio, yoga, and meditation into a unique blend that doesn't feel like working out, but is as strenuous as any HIIT exercise program.

Kwame's approach became so popular with his clients that he decided to start his own imaginary company, "Workoutopia", an online fitness coaching business.

At first, Kwame struggled to attract clients and generate leads for his business. He tried various marketing strategies, including social media, but found that they weren't as effective as he hoped they'd be. That's when he decided to try email marketing.

By this time, he had built up a small email list of around 750 subscribers. He sent messages to his list sporadically, without rhyme or reason, and tried hard-selling his training programs without much success. He knew there must be a better way.

Following the step-by-step checklist, here's how Kwame creates a successful email marketing campaign:

STEP 1: Define your marketing campaign objectives (15 minutes)

For this campaign, Kwame created a brand-new, 100% free, 7-day trial membership to Workoutopia. His goal is to convince 75 email subscribers (10% of the list) to sign up for the free trial, and get at least 15 of those (2% of the list) to convert to the paid membership.

STEP 2: Segment your email list for the campaign (2-4 hours if not already segmented)

Kwame decides to divide the list into three groups: beginner, intermediate, and advanced. Based on his previous interactions with most of the people on his list, he has a rough estimate of their fitness levels and sorts them accordingly.

For the rest, he sends out a few messages asking them to self-assess their fitness levels. Whoever doesn't respond gets put into the "beginner" segment, just to be safe.

(Later, he can create a dedicated web page where visitors can opt-in to the campaign and self-select which fitness level is most appropriate for them.)

STEP 3: Outline your email campaign journey (1 hour)

Kwame plans a 5-part email campaign series that spans 10 days.

Each email message includes three parts: a specific training method with a link to a video on the Workoutopia website where he coaches them through it, a client success story, and a call to action (CTA) for a free 7-day trial to Workoutopia.

Out of the five emails in the campaign, two of them are specific to the subscriber's fitness level.

That means he has to create two versions for beginners, two for intermediates, and two for advanced fitness levels. The remaining three email topics are applicable to all fitness levels.

That's a total of 9 emails he plans to create (3 for all levels, plus 2 for beginners, plus 2 for intermediates, plus 2 for advanced), each with a link to a 5-minute video. However, each subscriber still receives just 5 emails over 10 days, two of which are specific to their fitness level.

STEP 4: Write your email campaign content (15 minutes per email)

For each email in the series, Kwame includes one valuable fitness tip, a link to a 5-minute video on the Workoutopia website showing how to implement it, a unique client success story, and offers a sneak peek of his clients' success stories.

STEP 5: Create intriguing subject lines for each email (5 minutes per email)

Kwame crafts captivating subject lines for each email that accurately reflect its content and pique the reader's curiosity.

For the topic of stretching, his subject line is "Feeling stiff? Try these stretches for instant relief ".

A different email message teaching a light cardio workout has the subject line "This cardio routine feels like play, not work..".

STEP 6: Add strong calls-to-action for each email (5 minutes per email)

To entice subscribers to join a free 7-day trial for Workoutopia, Kwame offers three valuable bonuses that they can keep even if they decide not to continue with a paid membership.

These include a $97 "Fast Fun Fitness" video course, a $27 "90-Days to a New You" nutrition plan, and a $19 "Instant Relaxation" audio recording. By signing up for the free trial, subscribers get a total value of $143 in free bonuses.

Since the goal of the campaign is to drive subscribers to sign up for a free membership, he uses the same call to action at the end of all emails in the series: "Sign up for a free trial today and claim $143 in free bonuses".

STEP 7: Optimize your emails for mobile (5 minutes per email)

It's important to Kwame that his emails are mobile-responsive and look great on different devices and screen sizes.

His email service provider automatically formats all email messages to look great on any device, but he takes a few minutes to test each email by sending messages to his phone, tablet, and computer just to be sure.

STEP 8: Choose a send day and time for each email (1 minute per email)

For the 5 emails in the campaign, Kwame decides to send out one email message every other day over 10 days.

Most of his clients are early risers, so Kwame decides to send out every email message at 6:00 AM to try to catch them before they start their busy days. He figures after he has some data from two or three campaigns, he can vary send times to see whether that helps or hurts his results.

STEP 9: Automate the campaign (1-2 hours)

Rather than send out all these emails manually, Kwame chooses a reliable email service provider (ESP) to automate the entire campaign.

He uploads his list of 750 subscribers, tags them according to their fitness levels (beginners, intermediates, or advanced), creates an automated campaign, copies and pastes each of the 9 emails into a simple template inside the campaign, and creates a schedule for sending out 5 messages over 10 days, customized to each subscriber's fitness level.

STEP 10: Analyze the data and refine each message (1 hour per week)

Kwame tracks his campaign metrics, such as open rates, click-through rates, website visits, and conversion rates, for each email in his series.

He uses that data to identify areas for improvement and test new strategies to optimize his campaign, such as tweaking subject lines and changing the timing of his emails.

The happy ending to this imaginary story?

Using the step-by-step checklist for successful email marketing campaigns, Kwame Johnson was able to create an effective and personalized email campaign series that resonated with his target audience.

While Kwame ended up with only 67 free-trial conversions to Workoutopia (11% less than the 75 he hoped for), the good news is that 22 of those free trials converted to a paid monthly membership (50% higher than the 15 he predicted).

Strategy Snapshot For Creating Successful Email Marketing Campaigns

Successful email marketing campaigns require careful planning and execution.

A well-defined objective is essential, as it will determine the focus of the campaign.

Segmenting the email list based on demographics, interests, and behaviors allows for targeted messages that are relevant to each group.

It's important to outline the email campaign journey, including the number of messages, time period, and messaging topics, so your messages are cohesive and work together to create a larger story or narrative for your subscribers.

Compelling subject lines and strong calls-to-action are key elements to engage your audience and prompt them to take action.

Optimizing the emails for mobile devices ensures accessibility to a wider audience.

Automating the entire campaign using an email service provider (ESP) allows you to "set it and forget it", sending both current subscribers and new leads through your successful email marketing campaign from start to finish.

Finally, analyzing email metrics, such as click-through rates, website visits, and conversions, provides insights to refine your campaign strategy.

Take The First Step

To ensure the success of your email marketing campaign, it is essential to start by defining your campaign objectives. Spend 30 minutes today to define your objectives and set clear goals.

Do you want more sales for a specific product or service? Or solicit testimonials from your current and past customers? Or to create loyalty by nurturing your list by helping them solve their biggest problems for free?

Be crystal-clear on your objectives so that you have a way to measure them against the actual results over time.

By striving for clarity and consistency in your objectives, you can help your subscribers succeed while achieving success for your small business.

Chapter 9:
Why Content Engagement Should Be A Top Priority For Your Small Business

"Make the customer the hero of your story."

— Ann Handley

Why Is Content Engagement Important?

As a small business owner, you know that building a strong and loyal customer base is essential to the success of your business.

One of the most effective ways to do this is by creating engaging content that resonates with your audience.

Content engagement allows you to connect with your customers on a deeper level, building trust and establishing your brand as an authority in your industry.

By creating content that is interesting, informative, and relevant, you can attract new customers, retain existing ones, and ultimately drive more revenue to your business.

Here are just a few ways content engagement is important for the growth of your business:

1. **More shares**
   If your content is engaging, people are more likely to share it on social media platforms. This can help to increase the reach of your content and drive more traffic to your website.

2. **More backlinks**
   High-quality, engaging content is more likely to earn backlinks. (Backlinks are links from other websites that point to your website.) These are important for search engine optimization (SEO) and can help to drive more traffic to your website.

3. **Repeat visitors**
   Engaging content keeps visitors coming back to your website. By providing content that is interesting and valuable to your audience, you can create a loyal following that will keep returning to your website.

4. **More effective email marketing**
   Engaging content can help improve the effectiveness of your email marketing campaigns, resulting in higher open and click-through rates. By including links to your website in your emails, you'll encourage subscribers to visit your site and perhaps even buy your product or service.

5. **Traffic from guest content**
   Creating engaging content for other websites (such as writing guest blog posts, being interviewed on their podcasts, and participating in webinars), can help to drive traffic back to your own website. By asking for links back to your website to be included in your guest content, you can encourage their audiences to visit your site.

6. **Increased competitive advantage**
   By creating engaging content, you can differentiate your business from competitors and stand out in your market.

7. **Improved customer retention**
   Engaging content can help keep your existing customers engaged and interested in your small business, reducing the risk of churn.

"What Happens If I Don't Get Content Engagement?"

If your content is lifeless, boring, and otherwise not engaging, your business is in danger of becoming irrelevant, especially when your competitors are creating engaging content.

Here are just a few of the downsides to a lack of content engagement:

- **Weak social media presence**
  You will have fewer followers and interactions on social media, limiting your reach and audience.

- **Higher marketing costs**
  You may need to spend more money on advertising to attract customers, reducing your profitability.

- **Decreased market share**
  Your business won't stand out from competitors who invest in content engagement, reducing your market share.

- **Decreased conversions**
  Your website and marketing materials won't be as effective at persuading visitors to take action, resulting in fewer leads and sales.

- **Ineffective storytelling**
  Without content engagement, it can be harder to tell a compelling and memorable story about your brand, reducing your emotional connection with your audience.

- **Lower customer retention**
  Your customers won't have a memorable experience that stands out in their minds, reducing their likelihood of returning.

- **Poor customer segmentation**
  It will be harder to understand your audience and create targeted marketing campaigns that resonate with them.

===

Content engagement is a critical component of any successful small business strategy.

By creating content that is interesting, informative, and relevant, you can build a strong and loyal customer base, establish your brand as an authority in your industry, and drive more revenue for your business.

The Essential Elements Of Content Engagement

As a small business owner, creating engaging content is essential to building a strong and loyal customer base.

However, knowing what makes your content engaging can be challenging, especially with so many different approaches and strategies to consider.

Here are the 10 essential elements of content engagement that can help you create content that resonates with your audience and drives more revenue to your business:

1. **Relevance**
   Engaging content needs to be relevant to your audience and address their needs and interests.

2. **Originality**
   Content that is fresh, unique, and original can help you stand out from competitors and capture your audience's attention.

3. **Quality**
   Engaging content should be well-written, error-free, and visually appealing, conveying a professional image to your audience.

4. **Storytelling**
   A compelling narrative or story can make your content more engaging and memorable, resonating with your audience on a deeper level.

5. **Visuals**
   High-quality images, videos, and graphics can enhance your content and make it more visually appealing and engaging.

6. **Interactivity**
   Engaging content should encourage interaction and engagement from your audience, such as through comments, likes, and shares.

7. **Personalization**
   Content that is personalized to your audience's preferences and interests can make them feel more valued and engaged with your business.

8. **Consistency**
   Regularly publishing engaging content can help build momentum and keep your audience interested and engaged over time.

9. **Emotional connection**
   Engaging content should tap into your audience's emotions, creating a personal connection that fosters loyalty and trust.

10. **Call-to-action**
    Engaging content should include clear calls-to-action, encouraging your audience to take a specific action that benefits them, and, by extension, your business (assuming buying from you is in their best interest).

Content Engagement Step-by-Step

Here's an example of boring, unengaging content by "The Gizmo Company" (not a real company) that they posted on their (not-real) website:

"The Gizmo Company is a business that provides customized gizmos to gizmo collectors. We pride ourselves on delivering high-quality gizmos that meet the needs of our clients. Our team is dedicated to providing the best possible service. Contact us today to buy our gizmos."

Now let's take it through a step-by-step process to make their message more engaging, using the essential elements discussed earlier.

STEP 1: Ensure relevance (2-3 hours)

Through market research, The Gizmo Company identifies that gizmo collectors are concerned about the environmental impact of their collections.

To address this concern, they offer a new line of eco-friendly gizmos made from sustainable materials, such as bamboo and recycled plastics.

STEP 2: Emphasize originality (1-2 hours)

The Gizmo Company adds originality to their message by showcasing the most unique and creative gizmos they have created for their clients, such as a gizmo that doubles as a keychain or a gizmo that changes color in the sun.

They also offer a "Gizmo of the Month" feature that highlights the most original and creative gizmos created by their clients.

STEP 3: Focus on quality (2-3 hours)

They improve the quality of their message by highlighting their attention to detail and the high-quality materials they use in their gizmo creation process, such as aerospace-grade aluminum and durable polycarbonate to ensure their gizmos last a lifetime.

STEP 4: Incorporate storytelling (1-2 hours)

Featuring a story about how their first gizmo was created in a backyard shed by a visionary inventor who wanted to create a revolutionary new type of gizmo, The Gizmo Company adds storytelling to their message.

They also feature customer success stories and case studies that showcase the impact of their customized gizmos on their clients' collections.

STEP 5: Add visual appeal (1-2 hours)

The Gizmo Company hires a professional photographer to capture high-quality images of their most colorful and unique gizmos, which they add to their website above the copy to showcase their products and add visual appeal. They also add 360-degree videos that provide a detailed look at each gizmo from all angles.

STEP 6: Make it interactive (1-2 hours)

Through incorporating a live chat feature that allows their clients to ask questions and receive immediate answers from their team, The Gizmo Company makes their message interactive. They also add a quiz that helps clients identify which gizmo is best suited to their needs and interests.

STEP 7: Personalize the experience (1-2 hours)

Using personalization techniques, The Gizmo Company segments their email list and sends customized emails to their clients based on their preferences and interests. They also use personalized subject lines and greetings to make their clients feel valued and appreciated.

STEP 8: Maintain consistency (2-3 hours)

The Gizmo Company maintains consistency by showcasing a new gizmo every day on their website and social media platforms.

They also create an editorial calendar to plan and organize their content in advance to ensure they are providing valuable and engaging content on a regular basis.

STEP 9: Create an emotional connection (1-2 hours)

Showcasing the unique stories behind each gizmo and how it has impacted their clients' lives, The Gizmo Company creates an emotional connection to their content. They also use social media to engage with their clients and foster a sense of community.

STEP 10: Add a clear call to action (15-30 minutes)

The Gizmo Company adds a clear call to action by inviting their clients to contact them to learn more about their customized gizmos and to schedule a consultation to discuss their specific needs and interests.

They also offer a limited-time discount for new clients who sign up for their newsletter.

===

By applying these essential elements to their original boring content, The Gizmo Company has transformed their website message from completely uninteresting into a highly engaging and valuable content that resonates with their target audience and drives more revenue for their business.

SPECIFIC SCENARIO: The Office Cleaning Dudes

The fictional small business "The Office Cleaning Dudes", owned and operated by the also fictional Johnny Jameson, specializes in cleaning (you guessed it) office suites. Specifically, office suites in large, high-rise buildings.

In today's competitive marketplace, Johnny understands all too well that creating engaging content is crucial for his small business to stand out and attract customers.

This is especially true for service-based businesses like The Office Cleaning Dudes, which rely on their reputation and customer satisfaction to grow their business.

In this hypothetical example, we will walk through how Johnny and The Office Cleaning Dudes can apply the step-by-step process to create engaging content that connects with their target audience and drives business growth.

STEP 1: Ensure relevance (2-3 hours)

Through customer feedback, The Office Cleaning Dudes identifies that their clients are looking for green cleaning solutions that are environmentally friendly.

To address this concern, they offer eco-friendly cleaning products that are free of harsh chemicals and safe for the environment.

STEP 2: Emphasize originality (1-2 hours)

The Office Cleaning Dudes add originality to their messages by featuring their own proprietary line of eco-friendly cleaning products that clean better than traditional cleaning solutions.

In addition, they start offering a guarantee that nobody else in their industry offers: "100% satisfaction guarantee — or your next clean is free!" This risk-free guarantee gets them a lot of likes and shares on social media.

STEP 3: Focus on quality (2-3 hours)

Highlighting their attention to detail and their commitment to using high-quality cleaning products and equipment, The Office Cleaning Dudes start talking more about quality in their messaging.

They let everyone know about their microfiber cloths (to eliminate scratches on surfaces) and HEPA vacuums (to filter out all dust and allergens) to ensure a thorough cleaning and a healthy environment for their clients.

STEP 4: Incorporate storytelling (1-2 hours)

The Office Cleaning Dudes add storytelling to their messaging by featuring a story about how Johnny Jameson was living in his car when he started The Office Cleaning Dudes, and all he had back then was a bucket, a mop, and a passion for keeping offices clean and healthy.

They add customer success stories and case studies to their social media pages to showcase the impact of their cleaning services on their clients' businesses.

STEP 5: Add visual appeal (1-2 hours)

By using high-quality photos and videos that showcase the before and after of their cleaning services, The Office Cleaning Dudes add visual appeal to their message.

Infographics are created to highlight the benefits of their eco-friendly cleaning solutions.

STEP 6: Make it interactive (1-2 hours)

Incorporating a live chat feature that allows clients to ask questions and receive immediate answers from their team, The Office Cleaning Dudes make their message interactive.

They check their social media account daily to engage with their clients and respond to their comments and questions.

STEP 7: Personalize the experience (1-2 hours)

Using personalization techniques, The Office Cleaning Dudes tailor their communication to their clients' needs and interests.

Additionally, they start using personalized subject lines and greetings in their emails and newsletters, and offer customized cleaning plans that address their clients' specific concerns.

STEP 8: Maintain consistency (2-3 hours)

The Office Cleaning Dudes maintain consistency by posting new client testimonials on their website and social media platforms once a week (every Wednesday).

They also use an editorial calendar to plan and organize their content in advance to ensure they are providing valuable and engaging content on a regular basis.

STEP 9: Create an emotional connection (1-2 hours)

Showcasing the unique stories behind their clients and how their cleaning services have helped them achieve their business goals, The Office Cleaning Dudes create an emotional connection to their content.

They also offer tips and advice on how to maintain a healthy and clean office environment, which helps their clients feel empowered and informed.

STEP 10: Add a clear call to action (15-30 minutes)

Inviting their clients to contact them to learn more about their customized cleaning plans and to schedule a consultation to discuss their specific needs and interests, The Office Cleaning Dudes add a clear call to action.

They also offer a limited-time discount for new clients who sign up for their newsletter.

===

By following the step-by-step checklist, The Office Cleaning Dudes create content that is not only engaging but also effective in driving business growth.

Strategy Snapshot For Content Engagement

Content engagement is essential for your business to stand out and attract customers in today's competitive marketplace.

By creating content that is relevant, original, and of high quality, you can differentiate your business from competitors and drive growth.

Some benefits of content engagement include increased customer loyalty, higher conversion rates, and improved search engine optimization.

Conversely, failing to engage with customers through content can lead to negative consequences, such as decreased brand recognition, lower search engine rankings, and reduced customer loyalty.

The essential elements of content engagement include relevance, originality, quality, storytelling, visuals, interactivity, personalization, consistency, emotional connection, and a clear call to action.

When you prioritize content engagement and following the essential elements, your small businesses can create messaging that stands out and drives business growth.

Take The First Step

If you only have time to do one thing today to improve your content engagement, focus on ensuring that your messaging is relevant to your target audience.

Take the time to research and understand your customers' needs, interests, and pain points, and use this information to tailor your messaging to their specific needs.

This might involve creating messaging that speaks directly to their challenges, using language and visuals that resonate with them, or addressing their specific concerns or questions.

By prioritizing relevance in your messaging, you can create content that is more likely to connect with your audience and drive action.

So take a few minutes today to review your messaging and make sure that it is truly relevant to your target audience. This small step can go a long way in improving your content engagement and driving business growth.

Chapter 10:

How To Implement Website Search Engine Optimization As A Cost-Effective Way To Attract New Customers

"Google only loves you when everyone else loves you first."

— Wendy Piersall

Why Is Website Search Engine Optimization Important?

Website search engine optimization (SEO) is a cost-effective way to attract new customers because it helps increase the visibility and ranking of a website on search engine results pages (SERPs).

This means that when potential customers search for a product or service related to your business, they are more likely to find your website and click on it.

By optimizing your website's content, structure, and technical aspects for search engines, you can attract more qualified traffic to your site and improve your chances of converting visitors into customers.

Compared to other forms of online advertising, such as pay-per-click (PPC) ads, SEO can provide long-term benefits and sustainable results.

While PPC ads can deliver immediate traffic to a website, they can be expensive and require ongoing investment to maintain their effectiveness.

In contrast, SEO efforts can continue to generate organic traffic to a website even after the initial optimization work is completed, providing a more cost-effective way to attract new customers over time.

Overall, website search engine optimization is a cost-effective way to attract new customers because it can help increase the visibility and credibility of a business online, generate more qualified traffic to a website, and provide long-term benefits that can continue to drive growth and revenue.

There are many more advantages to website search engine optimization, including:

1. **Better brand credibility**
   When a small business appears at the top of search results, it creates a sense of credibility and trust in potential customers' minds.

2. **Increased local visibility**
   Local SEO can help small businesses reach local customers by optimizing their website for location-based search queries.

3. **Competitive edge**
   Effective SEO strategies can help small businesses compete with larger companies by leveling the playing field in terms of online visibility and reach.

4. **Higher ROI**
   SEO has been proven to provide a higher return on investment (ROI) compared to other marketing methods, making it an attractive option for small business owners.

5. **Measurable results**
   With the use of analytics tools, small business owners can measure the success of their SEO efforts and adjust their strategies accordingly.

6. **Long-term benefits**
   SEO strategies can provide long-term benefits to small businesses, as opposed to short-term gains from other marketing methods.

7. **Adaptability**
   SEO strategies can be adjusted and optimized over time to keep up with changes in search engine algorithms and consumer behavior, making it a flexible and adaptable marketing strategy for small businesses.

"What Happens If I Don't Implement Website Search Engine Optimization?"

As a small business owner selling products and/or services online, you can't afford to ignore website search engine optimization.

Here are a few of the dangers of not implementing SEO on your website:

- **Missed sales opportunities**
  Lack of SEO means potential customers may not find your website when searching for relevant products or services, resulting in missed sales opportunities.

- **Inability to compete**
  In a competitive online marketplace, businesses without effective SEO strategies struggle to compete with other businesses with higher online visibility.

- **Limited reach**
  Without effective SEO, you may be limited to a local customer base, missing out on potential customers from other areas.

- **Lower brand credibility**
  Lack of online visibility can result in a lower perceived credibility for your business and brand.

- **Higher marketing costs**
  Without SEO, you may have to rely on more expensive marketing methods like pay-per-click (PPC), print ads, or direct mail, all of which can be more expensive and less effective than website SEO.

===

SEO is a cost-effective marketing strategy that offers numerous benefits to small businesses, including increased online visibility, a competitive edge, and better brand credibility.

Website search engine optimization is both cheaper to implement in the short term than most forms of advertising, and much more effective for driving traffic in the long term.

The Essential Elements of Website Search Engine Optimization

In today's digital age, having a website for a small business is essential for reaching potential customers and driving sales.

However, simply having a website isn't enough. To be successful online, small businesses need to ensure that their website is optimized for search engines.

Here are the essential elements of website search engine optimization and its benefits for you as a small business owner.

1. **Keyword research**
   Understanding which keywords potential customers use to search for relevant products or services is an essential element of effective website search engine optimization.

2. **On-page optimization**
   This refers to optimizing website content, structure, and meta tags to improve search engine rankings.

3. **Technical SEO**
   This involves optimizing website speed, mobile-friendliness, and site structure to make it easier for search engines to crawl and index the site.

4. **Content creation**
   High-quality, relevant content is a critical element of effective website search engine optimization.

5. **Link building**
   Building high-quality backlinks to a website is an important element of off-page optimization and improving search engine rankings.

6. **Social media marketing**
   Social media can be used to promote website content and increase website traffic, making it an important element of website search engine optimization.

7. **Local SEO**
   For small businesses that serve a local customer base, optimizing for location-based search queries is a crucial element of website search engine optimization.

8. **User experience**
   Providing a positive user experience on a website is essential for retaining visitors, increasing engagement, and improving search engine rankings.

9. **Analytics tracking**
   Tracking website performance and user behavior is critical for measuring the effectiveness of SEO efforts and making data-driven decisions.

10. **Ongoing optimization**
    Website search engine optimization is an ongoing process that requires

regular optimization and updates to keep up with changes in search engine algorithms and user behavior.

Website Search Engine Optimization Step-by-Step

Implementing website SEO can seem daunting, but we've compiled this step-by-step checklist outlining the action items for the essential elements and the expected time investment for each step.

Follow this checklist to optimize your website and drive more traffic to your small business.

STEP 1: Conduct keyword research (2-3 hours)

Use a keyword research tool to identify high-volume, relevant keywords that you can target on your website.

By doing so, you can understand the search terms that your potential customers use and target them effectively.

STEP 2: Optimize title tags and meta descriptions (1-2 hours)

Use your targeted keywords in your title tags and meta descriptions to improve your website's visibility in search results.

By optimizing your title tags and meta descriptions, you can make it easier for search engines to understand the content of your website.

STEP 3: Improve website speed (2-3 hours)

Improve your website's speed by using tools like GTmetrix or Google PageSpeed Insights to identify and fix any website speed issues.

A faster website will lead to better user experience, increased engagement, and improved search engine rankings.

STEP 4: Optimize website content (2-3 hours)

Optimize your website content by using your targeted keywords in your website content, including headings, body copy, and image alt tags.

This helps search engines to understand the relevance of your website to specific search queries and improve your website's visibility in search engine results.

STEP 5: Build high-quality backlinks (2-3 hours per month)

Build high-quality backlinks to your website by reaching out to other websites in your industry and requesting backlinks.

By doing so, you can improve your website's authority and visibility in search engine results.

STEP 6: Promote content on social media (1-2 hours per week)

Promote your website content on social media channels to increase website traffic and engagement.

This will help to increase your website's visibility and attract more potential customers.

STEP 7: Optimize for local search (2-3 hours)

Optimize your website for local search by using location-based keywords in your website content and meta tags.

This helps improve your website's visibility in local search results and attract more local customers.

STEP 8: Improve user experience (2-3 hours)

Improve your website's user experience by conducting a website audit and making necessary changes to improve website navigation, layout, and load time.

By improving user experience, you can improve engagement and user retention on your website.

STEP 9: Install analytics tracking (1-2 hours)

Install Google Analytics or another tracking tool to monitor website traffic and user behavior.

This will help you to better understand how users interact with your website and make data-driven decisions to improve its performance.

STEP 10: Continuously monitor and optimize (2-3 hours per month)

Continuously monitor your website's performance and make necessary updates to improve search engine rankings and drive more traffic to your website.

By optimizing your website once a month, you can ensure that it stays competitive and continues to attract potential customers.

SPECIFIC SCENARIO: Vang Lan Restaurant

Anh Phan is the imaginary owner of an imaginary local Vietnamese restaurant called "Vang Lan".

She realized that her restaurant experienced a significant dip in foot traffic during slow periods between lunch and dinner, but she didn't know what to do about it.

Anh wanted to optimize her website to attract more customers during these slow periods. However, her site had never been optimized for search engine traffic. So she decided to enlist the help of an SEO consultant to implement website search optimization on her site.

The SEO consultant used our step-by-step checklist to optimize her site as follows:

STEP 1: Conduct keyword research (2-3 hours)

The SEO consultant used a keyword research tool to identify high-volume, relevant keywords that the restaurant can target on its website.

He found relevant keywords such as "Vietnamese food," "Pho," and "Banh Mi" that have a high search volume and are relevant to the restaurant's menu.

STEP 2: Optimize title tags and meta descriptions (1-2 hours)

After identifying the relevant keywords, the consultant incorporated them into the restaurant's title tags and meta descriptions to improve the website's visibility in search results.

This step ensured that the title tags and meta descriptions accurately reflected the content on the website and included targeted keywords to improve search engine rankings.

STEP 3: Improve website speed (2-3 hours)

To improve website speed, the consultant used a website speed optimization tool to identify and fix website speed issues.

He optimized images, reduced the size of the CSS and JavaScript files, and removed unnecessary plugins to ensure the website loaded quickly and provided a better user experience.

STEP 4: Optimize website content (2-3 hours)

The consultant optimized the restaurant's website content by incorporating the identified keywords into the website's headings, body copy, and image alt tags.

He also ensured that the website content was engaging, informative, and relevant to Vang Lan's menu to improve user experience and search engine rankings.

STEP 5: Build high-quality backlinks (2-3 hours per month)

To build high-quality backlinks, the consultant researched and reached out to other relevant websites in the restaurant industry and requested backlinks.

He made sure Vang Lan's website was listed on relevant directories and review sites to improve its authority and visibility in search engine results.

STEP 6: Promote content on social media (1-2 hours per week)

The SEO consultant created a social media strategy for the restaurant and began promoting the website's content on various social media channels.

He regularly posted about the restaurant's menu, promotions, and events to increase engagement and attract more customers to the restaurant.

STEP 7: Optimize for local search (2-3 hours)

To optimize the website for local search, the consultant used location-based keywords in the website's content and meta tags.

Additionally, he ensured that the restaurant's name, address, and phone number were consistent and accurate across all online directories to improve local visibility.

STEP 8: Improve user experience (2-3 hours)

The consultant conducted a website audit and made necessary changes to improve website navigation, layout, and load time.

He ensured that the website was mobile-friendly and optimized for all devices to provide a better user experience for all visitors to the website.

STEP 9: Install analytics tracking (1-2 hours)

The consultant installed Google Analytics to monitor website traffic and user behavior. He then set up custom reports to track website performance and identified areas for improvement, such as high bounce rates or low click-through rates.

STEP 10: Continuously monitor and optimize (2-3 hours per month)

The consultant continuously monitored the website's performance once a month, analyzing website traffic, engagement, and conversions. He makes necessary updates to improve search engine rankings and drive more traffic to Vang Lan's website.

===

With the consultant's help, Anh and her restaurant attracted new customers (employees from local businesses), and increase foot traffic during slow periods. Her website became a valuable marketing tool for her business.

Strategy Snapshot For Website Search Engine Optimization

Website search engine optimization (SEO) is a critical aspect of digital marketing for small businesses.

By optimizing your website, you can increase your search engine rankings, drive more traffic to your website, and ultimately increase your revenue and business success

Website SEO involves a range of essential elements, including conducting keyword research, optimizing title tags and meta descriptions, improving website speed, and optimizing website content.

Additionally, it includes building high-quality backlinks, promoting content on social media, optimizing for local search, improving user experience, installing analytics tracking, and continuously monitoring and optimizing your website.

Overall, website SEO is a cost-effective way for you to improve your online presence and attract more customers to your business.

Take The First Step

If you want to create progress with website search engine optimization (SEO) today, the most important thing you can do is conduct keyword research.

Using a keyword research tool, identify high-volume, relevant keywords that you can target on your website to improve your search engine rankings and drive more traffic to your business.

To take action, set aside 2-3 hours today to conduct keyword research using a free keyword research tool such as Google Keyword Planner or Ubersuggest.

Start by brainstorming a list of keywords relevant to your business, then use the tool to identify high-volume, relevant keywords that you can target on your website.

Incorporate these keywords into your website's headings, body copy, and image alt tags to improve your website's visibility in search results and drive more traffic to your business.

By taking this action today, you can make progress towards optimizing your website for search engines and improving your online presence.

Chapter 11:

How To Measure Marketing Results To Fine-Tune Your Messaging And Increase Conversion Rates

"If you can't measure something, you can't understand it. If you can't understand it, you can't control it. If you can't control it, you can't improve it."

— H. James Harrington

Why Is Measuring And Analyzing Marketing Results Important?

As a small business owner, it's essential to measure and analyze your marketing results to determine the effectiveness of your efforts.

Measuring and analyzing your marketing results allows you to make informed decisions about your marketing strategies and optimize them for better results.

Here are a few advantages of measuring and analyzing your marketing results:

1. **Make more money**
   By measuring your marketing results, you can see which campaigns are making the most money and focus on amplifying and repeating those campaigns.

2. **Learn what your customers like**
   Analyzing your marketing results helps you understand what your customers like and want, so you can create better campaigns, ads, services, and products.

3. **Find new opportunities**
   Measuring and analyzing your marketing results can help you find new ways to make money, like selling to new customers or making new products.

4. **Spend your money wisely**
   By measuring your marketing results, you can make sure you are spending your money in the right places to get the most out of it.

5. **Get better over time**
   By measuring and analyzing your marketing results, you can learn from your mistakes and make your marketing better over time.

6. **Make better decisions**
   Measuring your marketing results gives you information to help you make better decisions about your business.

7. **Stay on track**
   Measuring your marketing results helps you stay focused and accountable for your marketing efforts.

8. **Compare yourself to others**
   Analyzing your marketing results lets you see how you are doing compared to other businesses, so you can learn from them.

9. **Find the best ways to advertise**
   Measuring your marketing results helps you figure out which advertising methods work best for your business.

10. **Build a strong brand**
    By better understanding your customers, you gain valuable insights that help you create a brand that people love and trust.

"What Happens If I Don't Measure And Analyze My Marketing Results?"

Failing to measure and analyze your marketing results can have negative consequences for your small business.

Without measuring and analyzing your marketing efforts, you won't know what's working and what's not, which can lead to wasted resources, lost sales, and missed opportunities. .

Here are a few of the negative consequences of not measuring and analyzing your marketing results:

- **Missed Sales Opportunities**
  Potential customers are not being reached or are being turned off by ineffective marketing strategies.

- **Lack of Competitive Advantage**
  You are missing out on opportunities to differentiate yourself from competitors and gain a competitive advantage.

- **Ineffective Targeting**
  If you're not measuring and analyzing your results, chances are you are targeting the wrong audience or using the wrong marketing channels, wasting both time and money.

- **Higher Churn**
  It's difficult to identify customer needs and preferences, leading to missed opportunities to provide value to your customers, causing them to go elsewhere.

- **Difficulty in Optimizing Marketing Strategies**
  It's impossible to optimize your marketing strategies for better results and to continually improve your efforts.

- **Bad Decisions**
  Without the data you need to make informed decisions about your marketing strategies and business operations, you're bound to make bad decisions.

- **Lack of Accountability**
  It can be difficult to hold yourself and your team accountable for your marketing efforts and to track your progress towards your goals if you aren't measuring your results.

===

Measuring and analyzing your marketing results is critical for small business success. It helps you optimize your strategies, make informed decisions, and avoid wasted resources.

The Essential Elements Of Measuring And Analyzing Marketing Results

Measuring and analyzing your marketing results is a crucial process for any small business owner. However, it can be overwhelming to know where to start or what to focus on.

Here are ten essential elements to consider when measuring and analyzing your marketing results:

1. **Define your goals**
   Before you start measuring your marketing results, you need to define your goals. What do you want to achieve with your marketing efforts? Setting specific, measurable goals will help you determine which metrics to track and analyze.

2. **Identify key metrics**
   Identify the key performance indicators (KPIs) that will help you measure your progress towards your goals. These may include metrics such as website traffic, conversion rates, email open rates, or social media engagement.

3. **Set benchmarks**
   Set benchmarks for your KPIs based on past performance or industry standards. This will help you measure your progress over time and identify areas for improvement.

4. **Use analytics tools**
   Use analytics tools such as Google Analytics or social media insights to track your KPIs and gather data on your marketing performance.

5. **Track your customer journey**
   Track your customers' journey through your marketing funnel, from initial awareness to conversion and retention. This will help you identify areas where you may be losing potential customers or failing to retain existing ones.

6. **Analyze your competition**
   Analyze your competitors' marketing efforts to identify areas where you can differentiate yourself or gain a competitive advantage.

7. **Monitor trends**
   Keep an eye on industry trends and changes in consumer behavior to stay ahead of the curve and adapt your marketing strategies accordingly.

8. **Test and experiment**
   Test different marketing strategies and tactics to determine what works best for your business and target audience.

9. **Review and refine**
   Regularly review your marketing results and refine your strategies based on your findings to continually improve your performance.

10. **Use data to make informed decisions**
    Use the data you collect from measuring and analyzing your marketing results to make informed decisions about your marketing strategies and business operations. This will help you allocate your resources effectively and drive long-term growth for your business.

Measuring And Analyzing Marketing Results Step-by-Step

As a small business owner selling doohickeys, it's crucial to measure and analyze your marketing results to ensure that you're reaching your target audience effectively and achieving your business goals.

In this step-by-step checklist, you'll learn the essential elements of measuring and analyzing your marketing results for your doohickey dealership. More importantly, you'll be able to optimize your marketing efforts and achieve greater success in selling your doohickeys.

STEP 1: Define your goals (1 hour)

Determine your specific goal for your doohickey sales. For example, you want to increase sales by 30% in the next six months by increasing website traffic by 20% and email click-through rates by 15%.

STEP 2: Identify key metrics (1 hour)

You choose the following key metrics that will help you measure progress towards your goal: website traffic, email click-through rates, conversion rates, and sales revenue.

STEP 3: Set benchmarks (30 minutes)

You set a benchmark of 120 website visitors per month for the next six months based on past website traffic performance and industry standards. Similarly, you set benchmarks for email open rates, conversion rates, and sales revenue based on past performance and industry averages.

STEP 4: Use analytics tools (1 hour)

You decide to set up Google Analytics and social media insights to track your key metrics. Conversion tracking in Google Analytics is enabled to measure how many website visitors are converting into customers. A benchmark conversion rate of 5% is chosen based on past performance and industry standards.

STEP 5: Track your customer journey (2 hours)

By tracking where customers are abandoning their carts, you discover it's right before entering their credit card information. So you automate the sending of follow-up emails to encourage them to complete their purchases.

Additionally, you have your web developer provide clearer instructions during the checkout process and implement a progress bar to show customers how far along they are in the process.

STEP 6: Analyze your competition (1 hour)

By analyzing your competitors' marketing efforts, you identify areas where you can differentiate yourself or gain a competitive advantage. When you find out they're selling their doohickeys at $100 each, you see an opportunity to position your doohickeys as the luxury option in the market, so you increase the price to $300 to position them as a luxury model.

Additionally, you create marketing messaging that highlights the unique features and benefits of your doohickeys to further differentiate yourself from your competitors and justify the price.

STEP 7: Monitor trends (30 minutes a week)

Once a week, you keep an eye on industry trends and changes in consumer behavior to stay ahead of the curve and you adapt your marketing strategies accordingly. You notice a trend towards smaller and lighter doohickeys in the industry, so you start putting a spotlight on the portability of your doohickeys in your marketing messaging.

STEP 8: Test and experiment (2 hours a week)

Doohickeys are a volatile market, so you need to repeatedly test different marketing strategies and tactics to determine what works best for your business and target audience each week.

You decide to test different versions of your ad copy and images, and find that highlighting the unique features and benefits of your doohickeys in your ads leads to a higher click-through rate and conversion rate.

STEP 9: Review and refine (1 hour)

By regularly reviewing your marketing results and refining your strategies based on your findings, you are able to consistently improve your performance over time.

You review your lead conversion rate weekly and adjust your messaging and design as needed to improve performance.

When you notice that a particular marketing channel is not generating leads or sales, you allocate resources towards more effective channels.

STEP 10: Use data to make informed decisions (30 minutes)

The data you collect from measuring and analyzing your marketing results is used to make informed decisions about your marketing strategies and business operations. When you notice that a particular marketing channel is generating a high ROI, you allocate more resources towards that channel.

SPECIFIC SCENARIO: Inspirez Leadership Training

Melissa Cornwall Baker is the fictional founder and CEO of "Inspirez," an equally fictional leadership development company that specializes in providing executive-level training courses to top companies in the United States.

Melissa has always been passionate about leadership development and has dedicated her career to helping individuals and organizations reach their full potential.

After years of working as a consultant in the leadership development industry, Melissa decided to start her own company.

She founded Inspirez with the goal of providing innovative and effective training programs that would help executives and their teams improve their leadership skills and drive business growth.

Over the years, Inspirez has gained a reputation for excellence in the industry, and Melissa has established herself as a respected thought leader in the field of leadership development.

Now, with a strong track record of success and a growing demand for online training programs, Melissa is focused on expanding her business and reaching even more executives across the country.

Melissa has noticed a decline in Inspirez' online sales over the past few months, even though their offline sales are still strong due to positive word-of-mouth referrals. In order to understand what went wrong and take corrective measures, she asks her web developer to measure and analyze the company's marketing results.

Here's what happened when they went through the step-by-step process of measuring and analyzing marketing results for their online sales efforts:

STEP 1: Define your goals (1 hour)

Melissa decides that she wants to increase online sales by 20% within the next three months. Specifically, she wants to increase website traffic by 15%, email open rates by 10%, and lead conversion rates by 5%.

STEP 2: Identify key metrics (1 hour)

Inspirez chooses the following key metrics that will help measure progress towards the goal: website traffic, email open rates, conversion rates, and sales revenue.

STEP 3: Set benchmarks (30 minutes)

Based on the past three months' performance, Inspirez sets a benchmark of 1,200 website visitors per month for the next three months, with an average time on site of 3 minutes.

For email open rates, they set a benchmark of 30%, and for conversion rates, a benchmark of 10%.

STEP 4: Use analytics tools (1 hour)

Melissa's web developer sets up Google Analytics and email marketing software to track website traffic, email open rates, and conversion rates.

They also implement conversion tracking in Google Analytics to measure the number of website visitors converting into leads.

STEP 5: Track your customer journey (2 hours)

Through tracking website behavior, Inspirez discovers that many visitors abandon the site on the pricing page. They decide to simplify the pricing page and highlight the benefits of their executive training programs.

Additionally, they introduce a live chat feature to answer any questions potential customers may have.

STEP 6: Analyze your competition (1 hour)

Inspirez researches the competition and finds that some competitors are offering free webinars. In response, they offer a free webinar on leadership development to attract new leads.

They also tailor their marketing messaging to highlight the unique features and benefits of their executive training programs.

STEP 7: Monitor trends (30 minutes a week)

They keep an eye on industry trends and notices a growing demand for online leadership training programs. In response, they develop an online leadership course to supplement their existing offerings.

STEP 8: Test and experiment (2 hours a week)

The web developer experiments with different ad copy and images on their website and email marketing campaigns. He finds that highlighting the success stories of previous clients and their increased productivity leads to a higher conversion rate.

STEP 9: Review and refine (1 hour)

Inspirez reviews their website and email marketing performance weekly and adjusts their messaging and design as needed to improve performance.

They notice that the free webinar is generating leads and allocate more resources towards promoting it.

STEP 10: Use data to make informed decisions (30 minutes)

Inspirez uses the data collected from measuring and analyzing their marketing results to make informed decisions about their marketing strategies and business operations.

For example, when they see that their email open rates are higher in the mornings, they adjust their email marketing schedule accordingly.

===

Thanks to Melissa's proactive approach in measuring and analyzing Inspirez's marketing results, her web developer was able to identify the root cause of the drop in online sales.

They discovered that the website was not mobile-friendly, which was deterring potential customers from making purchases on their phones or tablets.

Melissa worked with her web developer to redesign the website with a responsive layout that was optimized for mobile devices. They also implemented a more streamlined checkout process and added customer reviews and testimonials to improve trust in the brand.

As a result of these changes, online sales began to steadily increase. Melissa also implemented regular monitoring and refinement of their marketing strategies, which led to continued growth and expansion for Inspirez.

Today, Inspirez is recognized as leading fictional leadership development training company in the industry, with a strong online presence and a growing list of satisfied clients.

Melissa is proud of the impact she has made in helping executives and their teams reach their full potential and drive business growth.

Strategy Snapshot For Measuring And Analyzing Marketing Results

Measuring and analyzing your marketing results is a requisite step for any small business owner who wants to succeed in today's competitive digital marketplace.

It allows you to track your progress towards achieving your goals, identify areas for improvement, and make informed decisions about your marketing strategies and business operations.

To effectively measure and analyze your marketing results, you need to define your goals, identify key metrics, set benchmarks, use analytics tools, track your customer journey, analyze your competition, monitor trends, test and experiment, review and refine, and use data to make informed decisions.

By following the step-by-step checklist, you can optimize your marketing efforts, achieve greater success in reaching your target audience, and ultimately grow your business.

Take The First Step

The most important thing you can do today to create progress is to define your "number one" goal for improving your website's performance.

That goal can be to increase website traffic, email click-through rates, conversion rates, sales revenue, or any other relevant metric that aligns with your overall business objectives.

Without a specific, measurable goal, it's impossible to know whether your marketing efforts are successful or not.

Take the time to identify what you want to achieve and how you'll measure progress towards that goal.

Set a realistic timeline and adjust as necessary based on your findings.

With a clear goal in place, you'll be able to make informed decisions and optimize your marketing efforts for greater success.

Take a few minutes today to define your number one goal for improving your online results and set yourself on the path to success.

Chapter 12:
How Continuously Improving Your Online Marketing Strategy Boosts Your Business Growth

"The road to success is always under construction."

— Lily Tomlin

Why Is It Important To Continuously Improve Your Online Marketing Strategy?

As a small business owner, you know the importance of effective marketing to attract and retain customers.

In today's digital age, having a strong online marketing strategy is more crucial than ever. By continuously improving your online marketing strategy, you can gain a competitive edge, reach new customers, and boost your sales.

Here are 10 advantages of continuously improving your online marketing strategy:

1. **Increased visibility**
   You can increase your visibility on search engines and social media platforms. This can help you reach new customers who may not have known about your business otherwise.

2. **Better targeting**
   You can target your advertising to specific demographics, geographic regions, and interests. This can help you get the most out of your advertising budget and reach the right customers.

3. **Improved customer engagement**
   You can create engaging and interactive content that connects with your customers on a deeper level. This can help you build stronger relationships with your customers and increase their loyalty to your brand.

4. **Increased website traffic**
   An effective online marketing strategy can drive more traffic to your website, which can lead to more sales and revenue. By continuously monitoring and improving your website's performance, you can ensure that you are getting the most out of your online presence.

5. **Improved brand reputation**
   By consistently producing high-quality content and engaging with your customers online, you can improve your brand reputation and establish yourself as an authority in your industry. This can help you attract new customers and retain existing ones.

6. **Increased customer insights**
   An effective online marketing strategy can provide you with valuable insights into your customers' preferences, behaviors, and needs. By analyzing this data, you can make informed decisions about your marketing strategy and better tailor your products and services to your customers.

7. **Greater cost-effectiveness**
   Online marketing can be a more cost-effective way to reach customers compared to traditional marketing methods. By continuously improving

your online marketing strategy, you can get the most out of your advertising budget and maximize your ROI.

8. **Competitive advantage**
   You can stay ahead of your competitors and differentiate yourself in the market. This can help you attract more customers and increase your sales.

9. **Increased flexibility**
   Online marketing allows you to be more flexible with your advertising and messaging. By continuously testing and refining your marketing strategy, you can adapt to changes in the market and stay ahead of the curve.

10. **Better customer experience**
    You can create a seamless and enjoyable experience for your customers across all online touchpoints. This can help you improve your customer satisfaction and retention rates.

"What Happens If I Don't Continuously Improve My Online Marketing Strategy?"

Failing to continuously improve your online marketing strategy can result in missed opportunities, lost customers, and reduced revenue. Here are a few negative consequences of not continuously improving your online marketing strategy:

- **Reduced visibility**
  A weak online marketing strategy can cause your business to appear less prominently on search engines and social media platforms, making it harder for potential customers to find your business.

- **Poor targeting**
  An ineffective online marketing strategy may not be well-targeted to the right demographics, geographic regions, and interests, resulting in wasted advertising spend and lower ROI.

- **Decreased website traffic**
  An ineffective online marketing strategy may not attract as much traffic or convert as many visitors into customers, resulting in lost revenue and missed opportunities.

- **Damaged brand reputation**
  Inconsistent or low-quality content can harm your brand reputation, making it harder to attract new customers and retain existing ones.

- **Missed customer insights**
  An ineffective online marketing strategy may cause you to miss out on valuable insights into your customers' preferences, behaviors, and needs, making it harder to tailor your products and services to meet their needs and preferences.

- **Wasted advertising spend**
  Poorly planned or executed online marketing campaigns can result in wasted advertising spend on ineffective campaigns or targeting the wrong audiences, leading to lower ROI and reduced revenue.

- **Competitive disadvantage**
  Falling behind competitors who are actively investing in their online presence can lead to lost market share and reduced revenue, leaving your business at a disadvantage.

===

By prioritizing the continuous improvement of your online marketing strategy, you can attract more customers, gain a competitive edge, and increase your revenue.

The Essential Elements Of Continuously Improving Your Online Marketing Strategy

Continuous improvement is essential for any small business looking to stay competitive in the digital age.

When it comes to online marketing, this means regularly evaluating and adjusting your strategy to improve results.

To help you achieve success, we've compiled a list of 10 essential elements that every small business should focus on when continuously improving their online marketing strategy:

1. **Data analysis**
   Regularly analyzing data related to your online marketing efforts is essential to identify areas of improvement and make data-driven decisions.

2. **Performance metrics**
   Tracking and measuring performance metrics related to your online marketing efforts can help you understand what works and what doesn't and adjust your strategy accordingly.

3. **A/B testing**
   Conducting A/B testing and experimenting with new tactics can help you find new ways to engage your audience and improve your results.

4. **Setting SMART goals**
   Setting specific, measurable, achievable, relevant, and time-bound (SMART) goals for your online marketing strategy can help you stay focused and measure progress over time.

5. **Industry research**
   Staying up-to-date with the latest trends and best practices in online marketing through industry research is crucial for continuous improvement and staying ahead of the competition.

6. **Competitor analysis**
   Analyzing your competitors' online marketing strategies can provide valuable insights and inspiration for improving your own strategy.

7. **Collaboration**
   Collaborating with colleagues, industry experts, and customers can provide fresh perspectives and new ideas for improving your online marketing strategy.

8. **Customer feedback**
   Seeking feedback and input from your customers is essential for understanding their needs and preferences, and identifying areas for improvement in your online marketing strategy.

9. **Innovative technologies**
   Embracing innovative technologies such as artificial intelligence,

chatbots, and augmented reality can help you stay ahead of the curve and take advantage of new opportunities.

10. **Flexibility**
    Being adaptable and flexible is crucial for continuous improvement in online marketing, as it allows you to respond quickly to changes in the market and adjust your strategy as needed.

Continuously Improving Your Online Marketing Strategy Step-by-Step

Improving your online marketing strategy is crucial for any small business looking to stay competitive in the digital age.

By following a step-by-step checklist, you can regularly evaluate and adjust your strategy to achieve optimal results.

To help you get started, we've compiled a list of specific actions you can take in just a few hours to improve your online marketing strategy and stay ahead of the competition:

STEP 1: Analyze online marketing data (1 hour per month)

Review and analyze website traffic, engagement rates, conversion rates, and other relevant metrics to identify areas for improvement and optimize your online marketing strategy.

STEP 2: Set SMART goals for online marketing strategy (1 hour per month)

Define specific, measurable, achievable, relevant, and time-bound (SMART) goals for your online marketing strategy to guide your efforts and track progress.

STEP 3: Research industry trends (2 hours per quarter)

Stay up-to-date with the latest trends and developments in online marketing by researching industry news, reports, and analysis. Use this knowledge to inform your strategy and stay ahead of the competition.

STEP 4: Reconfirm your target market (1 hour per quarter)

Understand your target audience's demographics, preferences, needs, and pain points to tailor your online marketing strategy and messaging to their current interests and behavior.

STEP 5: Analyze competitors' online marketing strategies (1 hour per month)

Track the online marketing activities of your competitors, including their social media presence, website design, and marketing campaigns. Analyze their strengths and weaknesses, and identify opportunities to differentiate yourself and improve your own online marketing strategy.

STEP 6: Collaborate with colleagues and industry experts (2 hours per quarter)

Connect with other experts in the online marketing field to gain new insights and ideas for improving your strategy. Attend industry events and conferences, network with peers, and share knowledge and best practices to stay informed about the latest trends and developments.

STEP 7: Seek customer feedback and input (1 hour per month)

Gather customer feedback through surveys, reviews, and other channels to understand their needs and preferences. Use this information to improve your online marketing strategy and better serve your target audience.

STEP 8: Create high-quality, engaging content (4 hours per month)

Develop and publish relevant, informative, and visually appealing content that resonates with your target audience. Use a mix of formats, such as blog posts, videos, infographics, and social media posts, to reach and engage your audience.

STEP 9: Test and optimize your online marketing strategy (2 hours per month)

Conduct A/B testing and other experiments to identify which tactics and strategies are most effective for achieving your goals. Use this data to optimize your online marketing strategy and improve your results.

STEP 10: Continuously measure and adjust your online marketing strategy (2 hours per quarter)

Regularly review and analyze your online marketing data to measure your progress and identify areas for improvement. Adjust your strategy as needed to stay aligned with your goals and adapt to changing trends and market conditions.

SPECIFIC SCENARIO: XYZ Company

Jake Robbins is a make-believe-but-still-hard-working handyman who has always had a passion for fixing things.

After years of working for other people, he decided to start his own (also make-believe) home repair company called "The Fixerator".

Unlike the Terminator, who mostly breaks things, Jake and his team call themselves "The Fixerators" because they can fix pretty much anything when it comes to residential home repair.

Jake has always been a hands-on person, but he quickly realized that in order to grow his business, he needed to establish an online presence. So he dove headfirst into learning about online marketing and started implementing different strategies to increase his visibility and attract more clients.

While Jake is happy with the results of his online marketing efforts so far, he also knows that he needs to stay current in order to continue to be effective.

He understands that online marketing methods can decrease in effectiveness every month until, at some point in the future (maybe as short as a year from now), they don't work at all. This realization has led him on a search for a guide to help him continuously improve his online marketing strategy.

One day, Jake stumbled across our step-by-step method for keeping his online presence fresh and new.

This guide provided him with the direction he needed to ensure that his online marketing efforts remain relevant and effective. Here's how he does it, with the help of his make-believe team:

STEP 1: Analyze your online marketing data (1 hour per month)

Each month, the marketing team at The Fixerator spends an hour analyzing their website traffic and social media engagement. They use tools like Google Analytics and Hootsuite to track which channels and campaigns are performing well and make decisions based on the data.

STEP 2: Set SMART goals for your online marketing strategy (30 minutes per month)

At the beginning of each month, The Fixerator's marketing team spends 30 minutes setting SMART goals for their online marketing strategy. For example, they might set a goal to increase website traffic by 10% or to generate 50 new leads through their Facebook ads.

STEP 3: Research industry trends (1 hour per quarter)

Every quarter, The Fixerator's marketing team spends an hour researching industry trends and best practices. They read blogs, attend webinars, and follow industry influencers on social media to stay up-to-date on the latest developments in the home repair industry.

STEP 4: Reconfirm your target market (1 hour per quarter)

Once a quarter, The Fixerator's marketing team spends an hour reconfirming their target market. They review customer feedback and surveys, as well as industry research, to ensure they are still targeting the right audience.

STEP 5: Analyze your competitors' online marketing strategies (1 hour per quarter)

Every quarter, The Fixerator's marketing team spends an hour analyzing their competitors' online marketing strategies. They review their competitors' websites, social media channels, and advertising campaigns to gain insights into what's working well in the industry.

STEP 6: Collaborate with colleagues and industry experts (2 hours per quarter)

Every quarter, The Fixerator's marketing team spends two hours collaborating with colleagues and industry experts. They discuss current marketing campaigns, share insights and ideas, and brainstorm new ways to reach their target audience.

STEP 7: Seek customer feedback and input (1 hour per quarter)

Once a quarter, The Fixerator's marketing team spends an hour seeking customer feedback and input. They send out surveys and analyze customer feedback to gain insights into what their customers like and dislike about their services.

STEP 8: A/B test your marketing campaigns (2 hours per quarter)

Every quarter, The Fixerator's marketing team spends two hours A/B testing their marketing campaigns. They test different variations of ad copy, landing pages, and email campaigns to see what works best and make adjustments accordingly.

STEP 9: Produce fresh, quality content (4 hours per month)

Each month, The Fixerator's marketing team spends four hours producing fresh, quality content for their website and social media channels. This includes writing blog posts, creating infographics, and filming videos to engage with their target audience.

STEP 10: Regularly review and adjust your online marketing strategy (2 hours per month)

At the end of each month, The Fixerator's marketing team spends two hours reviewing and adjusting their online marketing strategy based on the data and insights they've collected. They use this time to make adjustments to their campaigns, set new goals, and plan for the coming month.

Strategy Snapshot For Continuously Improving Your Online Marketing Strategy

Continuously improving your online marketing strategy is essential for the long-term success of your business.

By analyzing your online marketing data, setting SMART goals, researching industry trends, and reconfirming your target market, you can develop a comprehensive online marketing plan that evolves with your business.

Collaborating with colleagues and experts, seeking feedback and input from customers, and regularly A/B testing your online strategies will help you continuously improve and refine your marketing efforts.

Regularly researching your competitors' online marketing strategies, as well as staying current with the latest marketing tools and trends, will ensure that your business remains competitive in the ever-changing online landscape.

By investing a modest amount of time each month to maintain and improve your online marketing strategy, you can keep your business at the forefront of your industry and maximize your online presence for continued growth and success.

Take The First Step

The most important thing you can do to create progress today is to analyze your online marketing data.

Take one hour to dive deep into your website analytics, social media metrics, and email marketing campaigns.

Look for patterns and insights that can help you better understand your audience and how they interact with your brand.

From there, you can begin to identify areas for improvement and develop a plan for optimizing your online marketing strategy.

Don't delay — take action today to start improving your online marketing efforts and driving growth for your business.

Final Thoughts

Congratulations on completing the book on transforming your small business marketing!

You have now equipped yourself with a comprehensive guide to navigate the ever-changing landscape of online marketing.

Throughout this book, you have learned how to define your target market, conduct market research, and develop a marketing plan to promote your products or services effectively.

You have also discovered how to create a brand identity that increases customer loyalty and learned the formula for writing powerful marketing messages that grab attention and boost sales.

Furthermore, you have learned about the benefits of using social media, creating successful email marketing campaigns, focusing on content engagement, optimizing your website for search engines, and measuring marketing results.

Finally, you discovered how to continuously improve your online marketing strategy so that you never go out of date. Strategies and tactics change all the time, but if you follow the steps to continuous improvement, your online marketing presence will be timeless.

===

By reading the book, you have already taken the first step towards transforming your business growth.

However, the REAL transformation comes when you take action!

We encourage you to write down the most significant "a-ha" moment you had while reading this book and commit right now to taking action on it.

Seriously — put it in your calendar and make an appointment with yourself to follow through.

Remember, the journey towards successful small business marketing is continuous, and by implementing the strategies outlined in this book, you are setting yourself up for long-term success.

And if you have any questions, or need any help, visit our website at www.RapidBusinessGrowth.co to contact us. We'll help you get you on the right track.

Best of luck on your journey!

About The Authors

Dan Braun

Dan Braun has been an entrepreneur since grade school, selling homemade crossword puzzles at school between classes, newspapers door-to-door in his neighborhood, and helping his parents with their own small businesses.

Since those early days, he has founded or co-founded multiple startups that combined have sold tens of millions of dollars in courses, coaching, consulting, and live training events.

Most recently, Dan's focus has been on building FinishLine (www.FinishLine.io), a SaaS platform for rapid business growth.

Dan can be reached on LinkedIn at www.LinkedIn.com/in/xtraedge or via the RBG website at www.RapidBusinessGrowth.co.

Patch Baker

Patch Baker spent nearly 15 years serving our country and is a Service Disabled Veteran of the United States Marine Corps.

Patch is a serial entrepreneur, expert marketer, investor, speaker, and has acquired a unique set of skills through multiple acquisitions and business exits. His consulting clients range from Fortune 500 organizations to Veteran-owned start-ups.

He spends a majority of his time helping businesses create extraordinary results and growth within their respective markets. He also works diligently to connect Veteran and non-Veteran owned businesses, and individual Patriots, with brands and businesses which support our Nation's Warfighters.

Patch can be reached at www.PatchBaker.com.

Made in United States
Orlando, FL
30 November 2023